SEO Decoded

39 Search Engine Optimization
Strategies To Rank Your Website For The
Toughest Of Keywords!

Shane David

Before You Get Started

I'd like to show my appreciation to my readers by offering you a **FREE** upgrade to this book. It covers some of the most up to date SEO techniques that myself and my SEO mastermind group are using to gain TOP 10 rankings in Google.

Visit the link below to learn more.

TheFullTimer.com/SEO/

101 Epic SEO Resources Used By The Professionals

As a bonus for buying this book, I've also included all of the resources I use to do my SEO. I am a professional SEO consultant and I share all the resources I use to get the best results.

You can find these resources at the end of the book.

Table Of Contents

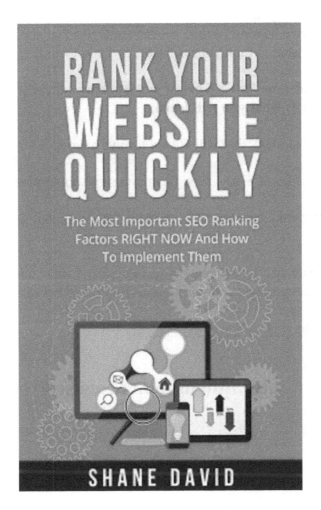

Wait A Minute! Rank Your Website Even Quicker With This *Free Gift*

As a token of my gratitude for purchasing my book, I wanted to give you a small, but very valuable gift. I've been doing SEO full time now since 1998 and I know better than anyone else how quickly things change when it comes to SEO.

But there are a handful of time proven strategies that always work and that constantly rank your website for the keywords that matter quickly.

You can grab your free gift below and implement these strategies today. **Here is what you will learn;**

* The ONE strategy that will almost always guarantee you high rankings
* The new rules of SEO – Google knows more about your site than ever before
* An instant rank boosting SEO strategy that you can implement in minutes

I also give away a lot of great content on SEO. I share all my latest tips and strategies and results, straight from the trenches.

<u>Click on the link below to get access;</u>

http://thefulltimer.com/seo/

Introduction

My first search engine rankings were back in 1998, (bless you Altavista), before Google was even a household name.

A lot has changed since those days and since the early days of Google dominance, but in some ways, there are a lot of similarities.

Search engine optimization or SEO isn't the complex beast people make it out to be.

It can become complex if you let it. If you've ever read any of the SEO blogs on the Internet or talked to someone selling SEO services, you would think it's akin to putting a man on the moon.

It's not.

It's about giving search engines and your readers what they want and in this book, I'm going to show you exactly how to do both those things.

You can't have good SEO without a good user experience, because SEO is more than just keywords on a page, it's about getting your visitors to take an action that you want them to take.

SEO isn't about tricking search engines and hoping for the best, it's about long term growth of your business, whether you are a small business, large corporation or someone who is running a blog and wants better rankings for their content.

(When I talk about search engines, I'm really talking about Google. Yes there are other search engines, but 99% of your search traffic will most likely come from Google.)

But who am I to tell you anything about SEO?

I have been the head of SEO for two digital media agencies and have been responsible for thousands of 1st page rankings for local & small businesses, large corporations, blogs, E-commerce stores, you name it, all over the world in many different markets and niches.

Who Is This Book For & What Am I Going To Teach?

This book is for anyone who wants to cut out the fluff and understand why websites rank. This isn't a primer or beginners guide to SEO, but it can be helpful for all knowledge levels.

This book mostly targets strategies to help you rank in Google. Google is the most dominant search engine and will supply you with 95% of your search traffic.

That's not to say the tactics in this book won't help you with all the other search engines, they will, but this book focuses on Google and on just doing good SEO in general.
If you are a beginner, you will understand what the most important ranking factors are. If you are doing your own SEO, you will know what to focus on first.

If you know some SEO but want to know the most important ranking factors so you can spend more time making money, again, this is for you.

This will also serve as refresher guide for those with an expert knowledge in SEO and you might even pick up a few new nuggets and in this business, that can mean a lot of extra money in your pocket at the end of the day.

So what am I going to teach you?

The ranking factors that will make the biggest difference to your search engine rankings.

There are literally hundreds of real and supposed ranking factors that Google employs to rank your website, but only a small portion of those will give you any sort of real boost or help.

That's what I'm focusing on.

The most important ranking factors so you can start to see results quicker. **I won't be teaching the basics of HTML or how to design with HTML or make changes to your site.**

Some of these strategies will seem like common sense, but those are often the most powerful.

I'll also be putting a rating system on each ranking strategy so you can tell the level of importance that I put on that strategy and you can determine which strategies you want to implement.
I'd recommend implementing them all, but I know time is scarce.

Part #1 – Keyword Research Strategies

Nothing happens without keyword research in the SEO landscape.

While keywords are playing a slightly smaller part in rankings these days, they are still vitally important and therefore it's vitally important that you learn how to do proper keyword research.

If you don't know what keywords are important to your business or what keywords are the most valuable to your business, you are kind of stuck in the middle of no where.

Choosing the wrong keywords can cost you big time. Trying to rank for the wrong keywords will cost you money and more importantly time.

So in Part #1, I'll be teaching you the following;

- Why relevancy is probably THE top SEO ranking factor and the one that affects your bottom line the most.

- How to determine (roughly) the competition of a keyword and how hard it is to rank for a certain keyword. Some keywords are almost beyond rankable and there are often better alternatives.

- One of the biggest flaws I see in keyword research is not using exact volume numbers for your keyword search amounts. I'm going to show you a very accurate way to determine keyword search volumes and how many visits you can expect to receive.

- I'm going to show you a simple way to find all the keywords your competitors are ranking for, including the search volume and even how hard it is to rank for said keywords.

- Commercial keyword intent. Unless you are running a blog and wanting to just go for sheer volume of visits, you will need to work out whether or not the keywords you are choosing have any commercial intent behind them, otherwise you are just ranking for fluff keywords of no value.

The goal of SEO is not sheer volume of traffic (not usually), but actual sales or at the very least getting your visitors to take an action that will lead to revenue for you. That can only happen if you choose the right keywords to begin with.

Understanding The Importance Of Relevancy

What do I mean by relevancy?

Google wants to rank the most relevant and helpful sites for the keyword or search term that was searched for. Makes sense right?

When you search on Google for a Plumber in Seattle, you don't want results for a bakery. No, you want to find a plumber.

That is relevancy in its simplest form.

The #1 key to search engine rankings and keyword research is being the most relevant search result for the keywords you are targeting.

Relevancy is needed in keyword research and relevancy is needed on your site as well, which I'll get to later in this book.

You want to find the most relevant keywords for your business or blog. I see a lot of businesses trying to rank for keywords that are only slightly relevant just because they think more keywords the better.

I was doing work for a client who was an electrician in Raleigh, North Carolina and he was absolutely set on the fact that he wanted to rank for the keyword 'Electrician North Carolina', even though as I found out, he only accepted work inside the Raleigh area.
While that keyword is somewhat relevant as he is an electrician in North Carolina, he didn't however offer his services outside of Raleigh, so the relevancy was completely gone.

'Electrician Raleigh' ended up being the keyword we really targeted for his site, but not without a struggle. Don't think more keywords at any cost, think relevancy.

What are the keywords that are most relevant to you? Really think about that. What are the keywords your potential customers are searching for to find you?

Same goes if you are writing a blog post. Let's say you have a blog post on the best eye creams under $50. You should be looking at keywords related solely to eye creams, not skin care or other beauty products.

Be relevant.

Be the most relevant search result for the keywords you are targeting and Google will reward you for it.

If you try and stuff keywords into your content or rank for keywords you are not relevant for, you will get no where fast and waste a lot of time and money and quite possibly get slapped by Google.

Relevancy is a huge ranking factor, it is THE factor in some ways, and there is no reason to go any further if you cannot grasp this simple but powerful concept.

You can't be all things to all people.

Importance Factor: 10/10 – Get This Wrong And You Are Dead In The Water.

Determining Keyword Competition

Not all keywords are rankable, not easily anyway. No matter what you do, sometimes it will take time to rank for the really hard keywords.

What I'm going to show you is how to work out what keywords are hard to rank for and what ones are not. You can then decide if you want to go after those keywords.

There are two things you want to look at when determining keyword competition.

Keyword competition being how hard it will be to rank for that keyword due to the competing pages already ranking for that keyword or keywords.

You want to look at page authority and you want to look at your competitions relevancy. Relevancy again plays a huge a part in rankings.

Just because there are a lot of large, well known websites ranking for a particular keyword, that doesn't mean you cannot rank for that keyword, especially if they are not as relevant as your page or site is and I'll cover all this in a minute.

Page authority is a metric created by Moz. Moz is an SEO authority blog and tool set. You should definitely check out Moz.com for more SEO reading.

Page authority is a score out of 100.

It tells you roughly how authoritative Google see's that page that is ranking. The higher the number, the more authority that page has in Google's eyes and the harder it will be to rank for a particular keyword if everyone of your competitors in the top 10 has a high page authority number.

So how do we determine competition using Moz?

First thing you need to do is install their free toolbar in your browser. You can do that here;

https://moz.com/tools/seo-toolbar

When you install this and do a search in Google for a search phrase or keyword if you will, you will see a bunch of numbers under your search results, that look like this;

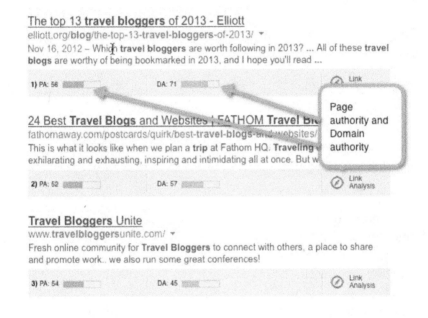

Image Courtesy Of Razer Social - http://www.razorsocial.com

It will give you two numbers. PA & DA. Page Authority and Domain Authority. You don't really need to worry about the authority of a domain when it comes to ranking for keywords, you are really just competing against the page.

I can outrank Yelp, Yahoo, Craigslist, Ebay, you name it, because of A) they have a low page authority page ranking for that keyword and

B) because I'm more relevant to the search query.

When it comes to page authority, I check not only the top 10 results, but the top 20 results in Google. I check page 1 and 2 of the search results because you are not just competing with the front page, you are competing with all the sites that are ranking.

Of course, you want to land on page 1, because anything below that is the friend zone. Nothing happens in the friend zone.

There is a funny quote that says;

"Do you know the best place to hide a dead body? Page 2 of Google."

So for all the keywords I've chosen, including my long tail keywords, I will check out the page authority of every site.

If all of the top 10 rankings are sites with page authority of 50 or more, that's a very tough keyword. It makes me question whether or not to go after it.

(Now, none of what I'm about to say is a hard and fast rule. Sometimes you can rank for really hard keywords, above competitors who have been doing this longer than you, but it's the exception, not the rule.)

That's not to say there might not be some really good long tail keywords that are an offshoot of this keyword that I could rank for.

Long tail keywords are those which are longer than what I call the seed keyword.

The seed keyword as an example could be;

Credit Cards

The long tail keywords from that could be;

Bad Credit Credit Cards
Best Credit Cards 2015
Best Low Interest Credit Cards
Best Credit Cards For Frequent Flyer Miles

So while the keyword 'credit cards' may be too hard to rank for, I could very well create a page or pages around some of these long tail keywords and rank for those as they would be less competitive.

By nature, the longer the search phrase, the less competition there will be.

I could even create an epic piece of content, 7500 words in length and target the keyword 'credit cards' but also sprinkle these long tail keywords throughout my content to get them to rank as well.

Back to keyword competition.

I will take all of my keywords and I will check the page authority for all the websites ranking for these keywords and I will note them down.

Now, page authority.

Anything under 31, I'm very confident on beating with just the on page SEO tactics I outline in this book with minimal backlinking or off page SEO work done.

I'd most likely be able to beat a 31 page authority site with a really good relevant page, long form content and some social media shares.

Anything between 32 & 51 I'm starting to think this is quite hard. So if the majority of the top 10 had sites ranking with this sort of page authority, it would give me some doubt.

Just because there are one or two sites with this sort of page authority shouldn't put you off, but if you are looking at result after result of this sort of number, you are probably trying to rank for a really hard keyword and you should look at long tail keywords that you could rank for instead.

Anything over 52 is re-donk hard to beat.

Now to throw a spanner in the works here.... none of the above actually matters too much if the sites ranking are not overly relevant to the keyword or search phrase used in this search.

If for example you are looking at the keyword;

Best Credit Cards For Frequent Flyer Miles

And none or very few of the sites are actually using that term in the title of their page or the majority of the page is not about that exact topic, these sites are not all that relevant and are ranking mostly because of their page authority.

You can beat these sites / pages all day long, regardless of their PA if you are more relevant than they are. Google wants to rank the most relevant sites for each search someone does.

This again is where relevancy plays a massive part in your success.

This is why I love the phrase, 'inch wide, mile deep'.

That's how I get most of my rankings for my self and my clients, by being the most relevant search result. Covering a small topic in A LOT of depth.

To determine competition, look at the relevancy and look at the page authority and while it's not fool proof, it's pretty close to it.

Importance Factor: 8/10 – Get This Wrong And You Set Yourself Up For A Longer Wait, But It's Not Impossible To Rank For

Exact Volume Only

One of the big mistakes I see people making when they do their keyword research using whatever tool they have in their arsenal, is looking at broad match search volumes instead of exact match search volumes.

Broad match gives you the search volumes for the keyword you are looking at for all the different variations of that keyword.

For example, the exact match being;

Womens hats

Broad match being;

Womens hats
Best womens hats
Cheap womens hats
Buy womens hats

You just want to look at exact match only volume.

There are two keyword tools that I use, they are;

http://SemRush.com - (Paid, with a free limited option)
Google Keyword Tool (Free, but you need a free Adwords account)

I have found these to be the most reliable keyword tools on the market. I use them both as they both can give different search volumes.

I find Google often over estimates the search volume for a keyword and I find that SemRush.com under estimates the volume, but if you take the middle ground of the two, it's surprisingly accurate.

Probably the most accurate search volumes you will find anywhere.

Now, search volumes are only half the battle. Not everyone who searches for the keywords you want to rank for are going to click on your website. You are competing in the top 10 with at least 9 other results.

What I'm about to share with you is the estimated click through rates (CTR) you can expect to get depending on where you are ranking in the top 10.

There are a lot of factors in play here however, not just where you rank.... including things like, how relevant your site is to the search phrase. (There is that relevancy factor again!).

What I'm about to share is from my own data from many different sites I own or work on and from the Google Webmaster Tools CTR tracker.

If you rank in the top position, the #1 spot, you will get around 30% to 32% of people clicking on your link when they do a search for the keyword you are ranking for.

Positions 2 & 3, around 15% & 10% respectively.

Positions 4,5,6, between 5% & 9%.

6 to 10, between 2% & 4%.

So you can see, the higher you rank, the more clicks you will get. That's obvious. But now you can work out to a higher degree of certainty how much traffic you will get from your keywords you want to rank for.

Be conservative, don't think you are going to rank in the top positions for every keyword. On average, my CTR is about 7% for my sites.

Importance Factor: 7/10 – Trying To Rank For Keywords With No Search Volume Is A Waste Of Time And Knowing How Much Traffic To Expect Will Help You Determine Whether To Go After That Potential Keyword Or Not.

Finding The Keywords Your Competitors Are Ranking For

Being able to see what keywords your competitors are ranking for and what those keywords search volume is, is a massive leg up for you.

This is perfectly legal by the way.

Why is this sort of information important? For a few reasons;
- It helps you find better keywords you might not have thought of
- It helps you determine how hard a keyword is to rank for
– If your competitor can do it, you probably can to
- You can see how much search traffic your competitors are getting

So let me show you how to do it.

Again, you will need to go to http://www.semrush.com

You can use the free option, but it is limited. You won't be able to see all the data and you can only do a limited amount of searches per day.

Sign up for a free account for now and if you need more, try it out for a month. It's very easy to use, you just put in the address of your competitors website.

If you want to look at all the keywords their entire site is ranking for, type in their address like this;

sitehere.com No   http:// or www.

If you want to see a specific page on their site, add in the above http:// or www. Or both

Select the country you want to search in. If your site is global, like a blog, use US, if you are only looking at ranking for a specific country, use the drop down menu to find that country.

This is great for local or small businesses.

Again, relevancy comes into play. If you are a business who only does business in one country, use that countries search results only.

live update TOP ORGANIC KEYWORDS (6) ⓘ			
Keyword	Pos	Volume	CPC
teeth whitening chicago	6	320	10.53
chicago teeth whitening	4	90	8.00
zoom whitening chicago	9	40	9.26
rembrandt tooth whitening	18	40	0.28
teeth whitening in chicago	3	20	7.50

Export   View full report

You can see an example of a SemRush search above. I was looking at a websites specific page who was ranking for 'teeth whitening Chicago'.

I can now see the top keywords that page is ranking for and the search volume.

It shows me their position for each keyword and the search volume and the cost per click if you wanted to advertise for that keyword with Google Adwords.

There is a lot more to this tool, but I suggest you play around with it yourself as the rest of it's features are outside the scope of this book.

Importance Factor: 7/10 – It's Not Essential You Do This Step, But It Sure Helps.

Creating Your Rankable Keyword Tree & Finding Easy To Rank For Long Tail Keywords

In this section I want to show you how to find keywords and also how to create a keyword tree. This keyword tree will be what you use as the basis of your site.

Everything flows from your keyword tree. In this example, I am going to use a fictitious blog and keyword set for that fictional blog, so you can see first hand how I do my keyword research.

The tools I will be using are;

SemRush.com

The free version so you can follow along, and;

Google's Keyword Tool

To use the Google Keyword Tool, you will need to signup for a free Adwords account with Google.

They require this to use the tool. You don't need to spend any money on advertising or put in any credit card at all.

https://www.google.com.au/adwords/

Simply signup for a free account and follow the steps. It takes all of 5 minutes to do this. You don't need the Google Keyword Tool if you pay for the PRO paid version of SEMRush.com.

I still recommend doing this step however as the Google Keyword Tool is very good as well and of course it's free to use.

Once you signup for your Adwords account, you can start using the search tool here;

https://adwords.google.com/KeywordPlanner

Sign in using your Adwords login details. You will come to a screen like this;

Keyword Planner

Where would you like to start?

🔍 Find new keywords

  ‣ Search for new keywords using a phrase, website or category

  ‣ Multiply keyword lists to get new ideas

📊 Plan your budget and get insights for keywords

  ‣ Get search volume data and trends

  ‣ Get click and cost performance forecasts

You want to click on the 'search for new keywords using a phrase' link. Now we can start searching for keywords. Where it says 'your product or service', that's where you want to put in your keywords.

Before you do that however, you want to change the location settings, maybe. Let me explain.

If you are a local business, you will want to change the location to your COUNTRY. If you are in the United States, change it from all locations to the United States. Don't drill down any further.

Don't drill down by state or city, which you can do, but we don't want to.

If you are in another country, select that country from the drop down menu. This will give you the search results from that country, not from everywhere in the world. Very important you do this step.

If you are a global business or a blog or don't want to target specific locations, leave this on all locations.

Now, for the moment, you don't need to change any other settings. In fact, I'd leave all settings as they are in the future, especially if you are new to this. Best not to complicate a simple process.

Now you want to put in some keywords into the keyword search area. This is where you will want to create your keyword tree and you will need to take notes.

I'm going to start using my example of my fictitious blog. I'm going to say I run a travel blog and I'm going to create an article on 'Things To Do In Chicago'.

That's my seed keyword. The keyword that all others will spring from, meaning, long tail keywords.

You always need to start with a seed keyword.

If you are a dentist in Chicago, then your first seed keyword would be 'dentist Chicago' or 'Chicago Dentist'.

If you were writing an article on the best vacuum cleaner, then my seed word I put into Google's Keyword Tool would be 'best vacuum cleaner'.

So my seed keyword is 'Things To Do In Chicago'. So I would put that and only that keyword into the search tool and then I'd click on 'keyword ideas'.

Now I have a list of keywords relevant to my seed keyword and their search volumes. I'm going to create my tree and then I would work out the competition for each keyword below.

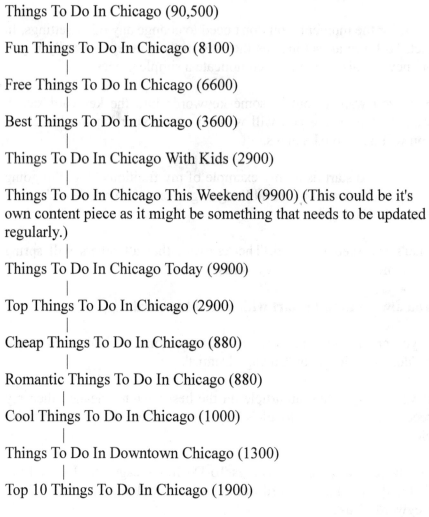

Things To Do In Chicago (90,500)

Fun Things To Do In Chicago (8100)

Free Things To Do In Chicago (6600)

Best Things To Do In Chicago (3600)

Things To Do In Chicago With Kids (2900)

Things To Do In Chicago This Weekend (9900) (This could be it's own content piece as it might be something that needs to be updated regularly.)

Things To Do In Chicago Today (9900)

Top Things To Do In Chicago (2900)

Cheap Things To Do In Chicago (880)

Romantic Things To Do In Chicago (880)

Cool Things To Do In Chicago (1000)

Things To Do In Downtown Chicago (1300)

Top 10 Things To Do In Chicago (1900)

I would keep going on like this until I found every relevant keyword.

I would then find all the sites ranking for these keywords and put those sites into SemRush.com so I could see A) who I was up against and B) more keywords I probably didn't even think of.

Get as many keywords as you can as you can cull later on. A lot of these keywords will become long tail keywords in your piece of content.

Yes, you want to rank for;

'Things To Do In Chicago'

But if you look above, you will notice that the longer tail keywords actually add up to close to what the main keyword gets in search volume.

That's why long tail keywords are so important. Don't just stop at the one keyword. You can work all these keywords naturally into your piece of content.

I would create one epic post or piece of content for this keyword set. If you create too many pieces of content on your site on very similar keywords, you will start competing with yourself in Google.

Google will rank the page that it thinks is most relevant and that might not be the right page for the right keyword, so try and group very similar keywords together into one piece of content.

I'd also run these keywords through SemRush.com as well to get the most accurate search number that I talked about earlier.

Another question I get asked often is search volume. How much or how little. This really depends on what your aim is.

If you are a local business and a keyword has 50 searches a month but it's highly targeted and one or two new leads a month would be a good new income source for you, then target it.

I am going to talk about commercial values of keywords shortly.

If you are writing a blog post like my example above and there are plenty of good keywords already, I'd probably stick with keywords higher than 250 searches a month.

You can write and try to rank for keywords with a small amount of search volume all day long, it will all add up and usually the small search volume keywords are easier to rank for. Another point to make is, there will often be very similar keywords in your keyword tree.

After I've done my keyword research, I'd go and look at the competition levels again.

I may find it's too competitive to worry about, I may find it's just right and I may find that regardless of the competition levels, I just want this article on my site to target these keywords regardless, which is perfectly fine.

Importance Factor: 10/10 – Without Keyword Research There Is No SEO And No Rankings. If You Get This Part Wrong, You Are Dead In The Water Before You've Even Begun.

Understanding The Commercial Value Of Keywords

Half the battle with SEO is often not related to trying to rank your website, it's about organization and truly understanding the value of the keywords you are choosing.

If you are running a business or you are trying to sell anything online, you want to choose keywords and search phrases that have commercial value.

Which keyword do you think has the most commercial value out of these two?

'The History Of Vacuum Cleaners'

Or
'
Best Vacuum Cleaner For Pet Hair'

It's the second one obviously.

The first one has no purchase intent behind it. Sure you could write a piece of content on that keyword and MAYBE someone reading that piece of content might click on a link and buy a vacuum from you, but probably not.

Someone looking to solve a problem, like example two on the other hand, is very likely to buy given the right choices.

You can even go a bit further.

'Best Vacuum Cleaner For Pet Hair'

That could lead to;

'Best Vacuum Cleaner For Dog Hair'

That could lead to;

'Best Vacuum Cleaner Under $150 For Dog Hair'

Every time you narrow it down, you are getting more commercial intent. Obviously, the more you narrow it down, the lower the search volume, but that's ok!

I'd rather 10 people coming to my site searching for;

'Best Vacuum Cleaner Under $150 For Dog Hair'

Then 100 people coming to my site searching for;

'The History Of Vacuum Cleaners'

Unless my goal is getting as much traffic to my site as possible because A) I've covered all the 'buying' keywords already or B) I make money from selling CPM ad space and for every thousand people to my site, I make $X in return from display advertising.

Look for buying keywords. This works for any business.

Importance Factor: 8/10 – If You Are Trying To Rank For The Wrong Keywords You Are Costing Yourself Time And Money

Part #2 - On Page SEO & Content SEO Ranking Strategies

What use to work with on page SEO no longer does.

What do I mean by on page SEO? This is what you do on your site, in your content, your page titles, your writing, your headings, your images, everything that goes on a page on your site.

Just like all aspects of SEO, on page SEO has changed dramatically over the years. In the early 2000's, you could put as many keywords on a page that you wanted and rank for just about every one of them, even if the content on the page had nothing to do with the keywords chosen.

You could even hide the keywords by using different fonts so readers could not see you were stuffing keywords all over your site.

This actually worked for quite a while and obviously didn't lead to the greatest results getting onto the first page.

Later on in the mid to even late 2000's you could still shove a lot of keywords on a page, you just had to do it more naturally.

Figures like 3 or 5% keyword density became a major aspect of SEO rankings. Trying to get your keyword into a piece of content as much as possible without 'over doing it'. You could rank shoddy little 500 word articles with high keyword density and spammy backlinks all day long.

Those days are over, mostly, thankfully.

On page SEO is more about good, useful content these days. That's not to say however that there are no strategies to use for on page SEO.

That couldn't be further from the truth.
On page SEO is HUGE. It's make or break, just like keyword research. It plays a massive part in how Google see's your site and where it ranks your site.

It's the easiest way to gain rankings as well because there are a few little tweaks that you can do that can have a huge improvement on your rankings.

So in part #2, I'll be teaching you the following:

- Why you need to think of each rankable page on your website as it's own separate site. This all comes down to how Google views your site and how they use page authority to rank your site and how you can use it to your advantage.

- The importance of optimized title, meta descriptions, H1, H2 tags. You can gain a lot of rankings with these small tweaks.

- Why keyword density no longer matters anywhere as much, but why using similar words in your content can help.

- Content length is huge, especially for bloggers going after more informational type keywords. You can't rank with 500 word pieces of content any more (not easily) in this context.

- A simple way to write content that is so epic it can't be ignored by Google.

- Epic content isn't always needed, sometimes just plain ole useful content gets the trick done. You will be learning why useful content might be the best option for your business and how to write it.

- The complete and utter importance of long tail keywords. If you are not using long tail keywords you are missing out on 50 to 100% of the traffic you could be getting.

- How simply linking between pages on your site can give your pages on your site a massive ranking boost, especially for less competitive keywords.

- Why proper url structure is still important for SEO and will be for a long time to come.

- The importance of images and formatting on your pages. It's all well and good to have great content, but if it's not easy to read, visitors leave quickly and that negatively affects your rankings.

Think Of Each Page On Your Site
As Almost A Separate Site Entirely

We've talked about page authority already in this book. We now know how to calculate page authority and why it's important.

That's why we need to treat each rankable page on your site with the same respect you give your site on the whole.

When I say rankable page, I mean pages you want to rank for.

There will be pages on your site for example, like your contact page, that you don't really want to rank for, for any keywords. It's simply a page for visitors on your site, not so much Google.

If you have a page on your site that you know you want to rank it for a keyword or keywords, that's a rankable page and this only applies to those pages.

Most of the pages on your site will most likely be rankable.

I like to think of all my rankable pages as a separate site entirely. Each page requires perfect on page SEO to rank for the keywords I want it to rank for.

If I clump all my pages into one or I try and rank all my pages for one keyword, I'll get no where. This is something I find a lot in my work with clients.

They have no idea what pages are rankable or they try to rank their homepage for every keyword they want to rank for, which could literally be dozens.

Of course they end up ranking no where quick.

Each rankable page on your site should have perfect on page SEO done to them. Each rankable page will target a seed keyword (main keyword) and a section of long tail keywords.

Importance Factor: 10/10 - If You Are Not Treating Each Rankable Page On Your Site As Well As Your Competitors Are, Then You Are Going To Rank No Where. You Need To Make Sure Every Aspect Of Your On Page SEO Is Tight.

Title, Meta Description, H1, H2 Tags

The first major aspect of on page SEO is the basics. You can see major search engine rankings for your site and your pages by simply just making sure you are doing these things correctly.

The very basics of on page SEO are;

Page Titles
Meta Descriptions
H1 Headings
H2 Headings

Let's start with page titles.

When you go to a website, the first piece of content you will see normally is the title of the page. The very first text you see in your browser tab will be the title.

These play a huge importance in SEO. Most people get these wrong and others don't do it 100% correctly, so I'd say by knowing the strategies I'm about to give you, you are ahead of 95% of your competition depending on your niche.

A page title describes to Google and your visitors what they are going to learn. It's the first piece of text you see when you do a search in Google and search results come up for all the listings.

You get a page title and a meta description in Google's search results. That's what you have to work with. It attracts visitors to your page and gives Google a good idea what your page is about.

Therefore Google weights page titles very highly. This is good and bad. You don't want to over do it with keywords or try and use page titles that are not relevant as you will get slapped hard, but if you do it right, you will get much better rankings and attract more visitors.

There can be a fine line and I'm going to use a few examples here.

Let's say you are creating a blog post on vodka cocktail recipes. You know your major keyword you want to rank for is vodka cocktail recipes as you've done your keyword research from part #1.

You would even like to rank for cocktail recipes if you could, but you know that 3 word keywords are usually much easier to rank for than 2 word keywords.

Obviously you want to get this keyword in your page title. It's exactly what your content is about and it's your main keyword.

I see a lot of blogs use page titles like this;

The Best Cocktail Recipes If You Have Vodka

Yes, the page title has the keyword in it, but not in the correct order. You should be using something like this;

27 Vodka Cocktail Recipes For This Summer

Not only do you need to think about getting your keyword (naturally) into the page title, you need to think about readability and more important, clickability. You also want to make sure, where possible, the keyword is in the correct order.

If someone searching for vodka cocktail recipes see's your site in the search results, but the title is not as appealing as those around you, then they won't click on your website.

SEO is just as much about your visitors as it is Google. There is no use ranking for a keyword if no one clicks on your site. Also, Google uses click thru rates (the amount of times someone clicks on your site in the search results) as a ranking factor.

You want great page titles for SEO and clickability.

So that page title above is enticing and it has the keyword in the correct positioning / order. There is also some thought that putting your keyword at the front of your page title sentence gives you a ranking boost.

I believe this 100% as I've tested it over and over. You still want to make your page titles sound natural, but if you can get your keyword to the front of the sentence, even better.

Again, don't try and stuff your keywords in an UN-natural fashion into the title. Don't do something like this;

Vodka Cocktail Recipes | Cocktail Recipes | Vodka Cocktails

That is bad for SEO and bad for clickability.

27 Vodka Cocktail Recipes For This Summer

Is clickable, it has the keyword close to the front of the page title and you are also in the chance to rank for 'Cocktail Recipes' as well, if that is what you are going for.

You can also use page titles to rank for long tail keywords. Long tail keywords are much easier to rank for and using them in the page title gives you a massive boost as most people use long tail keywords just in the content itself.

Here is another example. Let's say your major keyword you want to rank for is;

Best Electric Toothbrush

But you also know you want to rank for,

Best Electric Toothbrush Under $100

You know, that this is the second most searched for keyword when people search for best electric toothbrush, so you really want to rank for it.

Then you could have a page title like this;

Best Electric Toothbrush Under $150 – Our Top 10

It's relevant, the keyword is at the front, it fits in the long tail keyword, it sounds natural and it's clickable.

If someone searching for 'best electric toothbrush' saw your page title, they would naturally click it as it's relevant to their search and it's clickable.

Keyword positioning, relevancy and clickability. Those are the things you need to keep in mind when creating page titles. Also, you want it to sound natural.

The last thing you need to keep in mind with page titles is that they should be no more than 55 characters in length, otherwise Google cuts them off in their search results.

If they do this, you could end up with wonky page titles in their search results which would take your clickability down quite a bit.

Now, let's talk about meta descriptions.

Meta descriptions by themselves are not a ranking factor. They use to be, but they are not any more. If you are unsure what I mean by meta description, go do a search for any keyword in Google.

See the results?
For each result there is a page title in bold and text below that page title. That blurb is a meta description. This needs to be set on your page.

If you want to learn the basics of this, I'd suggest having a look at this link;

https://moz.com/learn/seo/meta-description

What I want to teach is not the technical aspects of how to setup a meta description, (this book isn't a book on website design, it's solely on SEO strategies), I want to explain why a meta description is so important even though it's not an actual ranking factor.

A meta description tells your soon to be visitors what they are going to learn on your page. That's why it's so important, because it draws in visitors from Google.

A bland, boring meta description won't draw in enough visitors, or a meta description which doesn't accurately explain what they will learn will result in them bouncing off your page back to Google looking for another site to visit, which in itself is a bad ranking factor.

So while a meta description is not a ranking factor Google looks at, it still helps with rankings in a round-a-bout way and it will draw in more visitors.

So how do you write a good meta description? First thing is to make sure its under 150 characters in length. If it's longer than that, Google will chop parts off and or not use it at all and use what they want to use, which is not always the best result for you.

The next thing is to make your text sound appealing, but not spammy or over hyped. Don't write it like an advertisement, simply describe what people will learn when they go to that page on your site.

Here is an example for a website offering chicken recipes;

Whether it's grilled, sautéed, baked, or roasted, this is your guide to the ultimate weeknight wonder: Chicken! With 100 of our best easy chicken recipes.

This draws you in, tells you exactly what you are going to learn and it's the perfect length. You don't need to worry about putting keywords into your meta description.

One more thing I'd like to add to this is a piece of code you should be adding to your site. It's a small piece of code, but it helps with Google to make sure your exact meta description is what you want it to be.

If your site is older, this is particularly helpful. This is the piece of code you should be adding in your <head> section of your website;

```
<meta name="googlebot" content="noodp">
```

Basically, it tells Google to not use the description that is being used at the Open Directory Project or Dmoz.com

Google pulls some data from this site and it is often old and not what you want as your description. You should put that code site wide.

I'm not going to get into too much detail on this as it's quite technical. All you need to know is why and how to do it.

If you want to learn more about this and meta tags in general, check out this piece by Moz.com

https://moz.com/blog/rewriting-the-beginners-guide-part-iv-continued-titles-meta-data-url-structures

It's a bit old, but still good.

Finally, let's discuss heading tags like H1 & H2.

H1, H2, H3, H4, H5, are HTML font tags that represent headings on your page. H1 being the biggest in size and given the most weight in Google.

Google uses these tags to see what ranking priority to give certain words on your page. If a word or phrase is wrapped in a H1 tag, they give this a bit more importance than a word or phrase wrapped in a H2 or H3 tag.

For the purposes of this book, I'm going to talk about just H1 & H2 as they are the biggest ranking factors.

When Google indexes your page, they look for quite a few things to determine what on your page is of importance. They are looking for keywords and phrases that your page is trying to rank for.

36

One of the ways they do this is to see what keywords you have in your title tags. H1 is given the most importance, but H1 is also your page title that we talked about earlier.

If you are using Wordpress to design your site, Wordpress automatically adds in a H1 tag to your page and it's your page title.

If you are not using Wordpress and you need to put in your own H1 tag, put it at the start of the page and make sure it's your current page title.

I find this works best. A H1 tag tells Google that the keywords in this sentence are the most important as they are the title of the page. This is what this page is about.

That's why you want to use your most important keywords and key phrases in your H1 tag. You should only ever use 1, H1 tag per page on your site.

H2 tags are used as sub headings. They help to break up the text on your page and make it easier to read instead of just having a wall of text, which is a big no no.

H2 tags are also the perfect place to put in your long tail keywords that you also want to rank this page for. In most pieces of content, you will have sub headings, these help the flow of the content.

They are also perfect to add in your long tail keywords we found earlier. If you did your keyword tree properly, you will have a main keyword for your page and a couple or more long tail keywords that you also want this page to rank for.

Let's say your main keyword is 'Chicken Recipes'.

Your H1 / title is;

27 Amazing Chicken Recipes On A Budget
Your main keyword is 'Chicken Recipes' in this example.

Now, your H2 tags could be this;

Fried Chicken Recipes
Grilled Chicken Recipes
Crumbed Chicken Recipes
One Pot Chicken Recipes

Those are the long tail keywords you want to also rank this piece of content for. So you should be using H2 tags to represent those keywords in your content.

Something like this;

Fried Chicken Recipes On A Budget

That would be your first H2 sub heading. Then you would put the recipes below that and do it over again with your other sub headings.

You want your H2 headings to sound natural and not be stuffed with keywords. Don't stuff keywords in any way, any where, it just doesn't work.

Get your keyword / key phrase into the sub heading naturally.

Importance Factor: 10/10 – Absolutely Fundamental To Achieving Great Rankings. You Cannot Rank Well Without Doing Your On-Page SEO Properly. These Simple Strategies Alone Can Rank Your Pages For Low To Medium Competition Keywords, Sometimes Even High Competition Keywords.

Forget Keyword Density, But Keywords Do Matter

Back in the day, you could 'game' Google's search by putting your keywords X amount of time in your content. That X changed over time, but most people were trying to get their keyword density to around 3 to 5%.

Meaning, for every 100 words, their main keyword would be in that content 3 to 5 times. It didn't matter to them if it sounded natural or not, they just plonked them in and hoped to rank.

And often they did.

Obviously Google got wise & they came out with a whole new host of penalties and updates that brought an end to keyword density and keyword stuffing.

But that's not to say that there isn't still merit to keywords and how they are arranged in your content. Good keyword selection is still very much key, but so is knowing how to use them to not only appeal to Google's algorithms, but also to your visitors.

There is no use having a page full of mumbo jumbo even if it ranks well, because those people coming to your site will just bounce straight back to Google and look for a better result.

It's a pointless tactic.

In this section I want to introduce you to a concept called, latent semantic indexing. Latent semantic indexing or LSI, is based on the principle that words that are used in the same context tend to have similar meanings.

It's all about context.

Google is smart, it knows that if you are writing about for example, on page SEO, people searching for keywords like, on page ranking factors, content ranking factors, etc, are relevant to your sites content, even if you don't have those exact words written on your page.

I'm not going to get too technical here, but by combining similar phrases into your sites content, instead of just using the same keyword over and over again, your page looks much more natural than a page that is just stuffing keywords and you are still getting that keyword ranking benefit.

It's about making your content look natural because it is. You don't need to stuff keywords into your page, your page just needs to be relevant and you can make your page look more relevant by simply using different phrases with the same meaning.

So when you are creating your content, think about similar phrases you can use instead of hammering the same old keyword over and over again.

Unsure what LSI keywords to use?

Do a search in Google for your keyword and let the auto suggest tool tell you what similar keywords people are searching for.

Importance Factor: 7/10 – This Is Something You Add To Your SEO Strategy When You've Nailed The Basics. If You Are Looking To Take Your SEO Game To Another Level, I'd Highly Suggest Learning All You Can About Latent Semantic Indexing.

The Importance Of Content Length

Over the past few years, Google and all search engines for that matter have put a massive importance on content quality and on content length.

Makes sense.

Good quality content is important to the user experience and that's what search engines are all about.

Content length doesn't always mean quality however, but content length has become a ranking factor in it's own right. Horrible, long form content is still bad content, but good, 500 word pieces of content don't have the same ranking power as good content that's 2000+ words in length.

That is a fairly general statement and there are cases where short form content does outrank longer form content, but in general, longer form content hands down beats short form content, especially for the more tougher of keywords.

Recent studies have shown that the average word count for a page ranking in the top 10 of Google is 2000 words and it goes higher, closer to 2500 to 3000 words for 1st place.

Don't believe me?

Go do a Google search for a medium to high competition keyword and look at the results. Still don't believe me?

Put those results into this tool;

http://www.seoreviewtools.com/bulk-web-page-word-count-checker/

This tool allows you to check the word count of all the pages in the top 10 search results. You will be able to easily work out the average word count and see what you are up against.

The days of cranking out short content hoping to rank for hard keywords is long gone. That's not to say that short content still doesn't have it's place, but if you are looking to rank for medium to hard competition keywords, your content is going to need to be longer and of a better quality.

Why would Google rank your 800 word piece of content when it can rank a 2500+ word epic piece of content on the same keyword / topic?

Not all keywords require long form content, but in general, long form content is going to outrank short form content. The ROI of long form content is much much higher.

Not only will you get better rankings, but user engagement will be much higher, in general.

If you are a blogger, long form content is a must. Local businesses can get away with shorter content as keywords are much less competitive.

Longer form content also allows you more opportunities to get in your long tail keywords, which I'll be talking about more in a moment.

The longer your content, the more chances you have of naturally sprinkling around more long tail keywords and long tail keywords can count for as much as 70 to 80% of your SEO traffic if done properly.

Long tail keywords are much easier to rank for as well as I've said before.

The other benefit of longer form content is it gets shared more on social networks.

Social media is becoming a massive part of SEO now. The more

Facebook likes and the more Twitter shares your website and your pages achieve, the better your rankings will be.

Importance Factor: 10/10 – You Are Just Not Going To Rank (In General) For Medium To High Competition Keywords With Articles As Short As 500 Words. Longer Form Content Gets Shared More, Ranks Better And Requires Less Off Page SEO On Your Part To Get Ranking.

A Simple Way To Write Epic Content Google Loves

Do you need to write epic, masterpieces of content to rank in Google? No, absolutely not and I will cover that in the next section.

Does epic content help your rankings?

Absolutely.

Longer form content that is of a very high quality ranks well and gets shared on social media a heck of a lot more, which in turn boosts your rankings.

But writing epic content isn't easy. If it was, everyone would be doing it.

In this section I'm going to show you a very easy way to write what I consider to be epic content. This tactic is perfect for bloggers or businesses trying to get their content shared and ranked.

The first thing we need to do is define what 'epic content' is.

Epic content is something that covers a topic in a way no one else has. It's content that people want to read and share. That's an important distinction. General readers and influencers in your industry should want to share this content.

When I go to write epic content, the first thought in my mind is this;

Inch Deep, Mile Wide.

What do I mean by that?

I mean you should be covering a very specific topic in a great level of detail. For example, SEO in general is too broad of a topic. Local SEO however would make a perfect fit.

A complete guide to doing Local SEO for your business would have everyone from small business owners to people who offer Local SEO services linking back to you and sharing your content.

You want a very defined audience for your epic content and you want to cover it in MASSIVE depth.

So how do you know what you should be covering and what you should be writing in your epic content?

The easiest way is to find what is doing well now and completely blowing it out of the water.

I'll be more specific in a moment, but if you can find an epic piece of content in your industry, and you can see it's being shared and it's ranking well, create something similar but even more epic, even more in depth, even more step by step.

Let's get more specific.

Now let's say you run a blog on poker. You cover topics for beginners and intermediates alike.

You monetize your blog with advertisements and you also sell information products on the topic of poker and becoming a better poker player.

Now you want to create an epic piece of content so you can sell more products, but you are unsure of what to create it on.

This is where BuzzSumo.com comes into play.

Http://www.buzzsumo.com

BuzzSumo looks at the popularity of content based on it's social shares. You can type in a keyword into the BuzzSumo search box and it will display the most socially shared pieces of content based around that keyword.

This tool shaves hours off your research time.

Going back to our example of our poker blog. We want to create something epic and we are not sure what we want to cover.

So I'll type something like;

Poker Strategies

Into the BuzzSumo search box and see what the results come back as. This is what I found, in one of the top 3 spots.

"How to Bet in Poker Tournaments: A Guide to Sizing Your Bets Like a Pro"

It has over 1000 shares on Facebook and Twitter so I know it's popular. This would make a great topic for a piece of content on our imaginary blog.

This works in any industry and on pretty much any topic.

With our example above, I'd be looking at creating something very similar. I'd also be looking at in the future, a piece of content on betting in cash games as well, but that's a future article.

So how can we create a better piece of content than this piece?

Well, let's look at it's weaknesses shall we?

The first thing I check for is content length. Using the word count tool I talked about above, I can see it's only around 1500 words in length.

We know we can dominate this piece of content with a larger more in depth piece of content.

What I'd do next is a Google search on this very topic.

'Bet sizing in tournaments'

I'd find all the pieces of content I could on this topic, read them all and work out what they cover that this article does not.

After doing a bit of this research myself for you, I found what was lacking was information on bet sizing later in tournaments.

The bet sizing strategies early on are vastly different to later in a tournament. I'd be writing a complete article on early, mid and late bet sizing.

I'd be writing about early, mid and late bet sizing, in regards to position at the table, in different parts of the tournaments stages.

I'd be talking about the different type of online tournaments, IE, regular paced tournaments and turbo's which are much quicker. I'd also be writing about knockout tournaments and how that should affect your bet sizing.

I'd also talk about the bubble.

Being on the bubble means you are close to getting into a paying position. If you bust before the bubble you don't win anything, if you bust after the bubble you are in the money and the prize pool increases from there on out.

Right now this article covers a few good examples of bet sizing in a pretty easy to read format, but you could completely blow it out of the water by combining all the different topics other people have talked about in their content.

I'd read everything I could and make notes of what I want to cover extra over the top of what this piece of content we found on BuzzSumo had.

Go look at forums and ask what they would like to learn about bet sizing. People will give you answers. All of this information about research is applicable to any industry on just about any topic.

I'd make this piece of content on bet sizing in poker tournaments the most step by step, in depth content I could possible write. I would leave no stone UN-turned.

In a later section of this book, I'll be showing you a way on how to get your epic content shared widely on social media.

Importance Factor: 8/10 – You Don't Need Epic Content To Rank Well In Google, But It Doesn't Hurt You Either. Epic Content Makes Most Sense For Bloggers Looking To Rank For Very Difficult Keywords And To Also Build Their Brand.

A Simple Way To Write Useful / Relevant Content Google Loves

We've talked about epic content, now let's talk about a more measured way of writing content that ranks well in Google. This is what I'd suggest most of you do, especially small businesses and businesses in general.

You don't need epic content to rank in Google. You just need content that is better than what is already out there already and luckily for you, most content is borderline rubbish.

So what do I mean by relevant, useful content?

First, let's start with content length. By default, I'm going to say that you should be aiming for at least 1500 words in length for any page you want to rank for.

Especially if the keywords are even remotely more difficult than super easy. People will disagree and there are exceptions to this rule, but why do less than your competitors?

That sounds like a quick way to fail to me. It's very frustrating talking to a client about content length and they say they don't see the need to pay for better, longer content.

Content is content.

That statement could not be more wrong.

How do you think you are going to out rank your competitors by doing less than they are? By default you should be doing 2 to 3 times as much as they are.

By default.

Aiming for average is going to get you below average results. Your content doesn't have to be spectacular, it just has to be useful.

Google itself often ranks more useful content over epic masterpieces all the time. The reason you write epic content is to get social shares and brand yourself as an expert.

If all you want is the rankings, useful / relevant content will get you there and the minimum you should be aiming for is 1500 words and upwards to 2500 for more competitive keywords.

So what is useful content?
Useful content answers the question of the keyword you are targeting. Are you a local business offering teeth whitening in Denver?

Are you targeting a keyword like 'best teeth whitening in Denver'?

Well than;

'Yes, we believe we are the best teeth whitening service in Denver, we've been in business X amount of years and this is how we do our service and this is how we differ over our competitors.'

Expand on that for 1500 words and you have very useful content.

Google wants to rank the most relevant search results. Relevancy is HUGE. To be able to rank for the keywords you want to rank for and be profitable from the visitors coming to your site, you need to be the MOST RELEVANT search result.

Bare minimum.

Now you throw in long form content, great on page SEO and some basic off page SEO and you have yourself a top 10 ranking page for a keyword that means something to your business.

Useful content answers the question of the keyword searched for. No more, no less. It does it with no fluff and no ambiguity.

It's just useful and it ranks because your page is relevant to the keyword you are trying to rank for.

There is no magic formula here, just make your content useful and relevant and watch the length of your content.

Importance Factor: 10/10 – Useful Content Is The Bedrock Of SEO. There Is No SEO Without Useful Content. There Is No Internet Without Useful Content.

Long Tail Keywords Are HUGELY Important (The Backdoor Of SEO)

I've already touched a bit on long tail keywords in the section on keyword research at the beginning of this book, but they are so important to SEO success that I wanted to talk a bit more in depth about them and how to use them in your content.

Long tail keywords are keywords that come from your seed keywords. Your main seed keyword could be;
'Content Marketing'

Long tail keywords would be something like;

Content marketing strategy
Content marketing on a budget
Content marketing plan template

They are longer versions of your main keyword that make sense to the piece of content you are going to be writing.

Long tail keywords can account for upwards of 50% to 80% of your SEO traffic. While ranking for your big keyword is great, you are missing out on most of the traffic you could be getting if you are not targeting long tail keywords.

Long tail keywords are also more profitable, in so far as they are tighter and more specific, meaning those people searching for that specific long tail keyword are looking for something very specific and usually are a higher quality search.

You can create pages on your site around long tail keywords or you can add them into longer pieces of epic or useful content that you write for your site.

The longer your content length, the more long tail keywords you can naturally sprinkle through your content.

So what is the best way to use long tail keywords in your content? This is how I use them when I'm writing content.

. I use them as H2 sub headings
. I sprinkle them naturally into my content
. I rename my images after them
. If I can, I get them into my title

Long tail keywords are best used in your H2 sub headings, which I have talked about somewhat already. Long tail keywords by nature are easier to rank for, so by putting them into your H2 sub headings, that is often enough SEO juice to rank for them when it comes to on page SEO.

Most of your competitors are either a) not using long tail keywords or b) not giving them the value they should be. You obviously don't want to stuff your content full of H2 sub headings, but there is no harm is using 3 or 4 H2 subheadings in a 2000 word piece of content.

The key here is to naturally introduce them into your content. Don't just plonk them in. If it's obvious you put these sub headings in just to get your long tail keywords in, that's a no no.

It should not be obvious that you are using any keywords at all in your content.

Sub headings or not.

Sometimes your long tail keywords don't fit in all that naturally as is, so adding an extra word or two is not a big deal.

Remember how we talked about latent semantic indexing?
If your keyword is;

Teeth Whitening Denver

It's fine to use Teeth whitening in Denver as your phrase. You can see I added an 'in' there.

You should also be sprinkling them or a variance of your long tail keywords naturally into your content.

This doesn't need to be a set % or anything even close to that, just something to remember when you are writing your content.

Make your content the most relevant, best content for the keywords you are trying to rank for. Answer the questions people have with their search results and remember to sprinkle in your long tail keywords as you go.

It's all about looking natural because it is natural.

Importance Factor: 9/10 – You Really Should Be Using Long Tail Keywords In Your Content. It Takes Very Little Extra Time And The Pay Off Is Potentially Huge.

How Internal Linking Can Massively Increase Your Rankings

Most people think that backlinks from other sites are the only type of links that increase your pages rankings. Not true at all.

Interlinking or internal linking can also help you rank your pages higher. Google looks at all links when it evaluates the ranking strength of a page, including the links you create yourself to your own pages.

What do I mean by internal linking?

Let's say you have a piece of content on your site about the best poker starting hands. In that piece of content you also mention something about the right amount to bet when raising a hand, and you just happen to have another article on that topic on your site, so you link naturally to that other piece of content inside this piece of content on the best poker starting hands.

Bam, you have an internal link, which will pass some of the ranking power of that page onto your other page. This works best when you interlink between an older article to a newer article.

It gives the newer article a boost.

So how do you go about doing this the right and most optimal way?

Obviously you don't want to turn each of your articles or pieces of content into link farms, you want to do this selectively.

You also need to make sure you don't over do the keywords in your anchor text. An anchor text is the words you wrap in your link. For example;

Teeth Whitening Denver

The anchor text for that link is Teeth Whitening Denver. You really should not be using blatant keywords in your anchor text, especially if it doesn't read naturally.

Let me give you an example with the poker blog. I am writing an article on starting hands and I want to link to another article on my site.

'When it comes to starting hands, you really should only be playing the top 10% early in a tournament or out of position. When it comes to **what bet sizing you should be using**, I would recommend 2.5 x BB as a good starting point."

Can you see how natural that link looks? Google has cracked down on anchor text keyword stuffing for off page SEO, IE, from backlinks from other peoples sites and as well with your own internal linking.

You want your link to look natural, because it is!

A good suggestion is to bold the link as well so it stands out more for readers to click on as that is ultimately the goal.

Our goal should always be to get readers to read more of our content. SEO is secondary in this case, it just happens that internal linking also has major importance with SEO.

Win/Win.

I would normally have no more than 2 or 3 internal links per piece of content in that 1500 to 2500 word range.

When you create a new piece of content, you should go back over your old content, especially content that is ranking well and look for places to link internally to this new piece of content.

Obviously, make sure the two pieces of content are at least somewhat relevant to each other, or it won't look natural to readers.

I try and find at least two or three pieces of old content to link to my new piece of content. Don't try and link to the new piece of content 2 or 3 times in the same piece of old content, look for 2 or 3 different pieces of content and make sure it's a relevant link.

Links from more, relevant pages is what we are after, not just more links for the sake of it.

Importance Factor: 8/10 – Internal Linking Can Give Your Newer Pages On Your Site Quite A Big SEO Boost So I Always Recommend Doing It When You Can. It's Not Essential But You Are Missing Out On Some Easy Rank Boosting Not Employing This Strategy.

Urls!

When you are creating your site or adding in a new piece of content or a new page to your site, you get to set the URL.

What do I mean by that?

Let's say you have an article targeting the keyword 'Indoor Golf Simulator'. When you create that article, do you want the URL for that article to be;

YourSiteHere.com/113hj-324/

Or

YourSiteHere.com/indoor-golf-simulator/

(Before I go any further, I should mention, this book won't be teaching you how to create sites, do HTML, change settings on your site, etc, this is purely giving you SEO knowledge. There are plenty of free resources available if you Google your question.)

If you chose the bottom example, you would be right, with a caveat. Trying to keyword stuff in your URLs is just as bad as keyword stuffing in your title or your content.

Google has given less weight to URLs with keywords in them. So you won't get the same benefit you would have had 5 years ago.

That's not to say you don't get some benefit, because you still do. You just want to do this smart.

I, myself am quite happy using my main keyword in my URL, like the example above. Other people suggest using your title or a snippet of your title as your URL to make it look more natural.

For example:

YourSiteHere.com/our-favorite-indoor-golf-simulators/

It still has the keyword in it, but it does look more natural. I'd recommend using either or, but never the first example which is gibberish.

Why?

Because A) it gives you no SEO benefit and B) it's bad for readers. It looks spammy, it's hard to remember and it just doesn't flow well.

Importance Factor: 7/10 – 5 Years Ago I Would Have Given This A 10/10, Not So Much These Days, But You Still Should Be Creating User Friendly URLs At The Very Least.

Images / Media & Formatting

You are probably asking, how can images and formatting improve my SEO? It's a good question and there is an even better answer. (Hopefully!).

Images can be used for two purposes.

A) Keyword rich file names (not such a big deal any more for SEO purposes) and B) making your page look good to your visitors.

Same goes with other media like video and formatting. There is nothing worse then when you are browsing and you come to a site that is just a wall of text.

That text could be super relevant to your search result, but the chances of you reading more than a few lines is slim to none.

So yes, images, media and formatting play a big role in SEO.

Google measures statistics like how long someone stays on your site and whether or not they bounce straight back to find another site in their search results.

If people are coming to your site and pressing the back button immediately, that's a huge sign to Google that something is wrong with your page / site in general.

There is no use having the best content in the world if no one can or wants to read it. So what can you do to get the formatting right?

First thing I do is I always make sure to have at least one image per 1000 words of content. Just something to break up the wall of text.

You can have the image either standalone or have it formatted / wrapped into the text itself.

Just make sure the images you use are relevant to the content on the page. If you want to find good royalty free photo's that don't cost a fortune, you can go to;

PhotoDune.net

Taking just any photo from the Internet is against copyright law. You might not get caught, but you also might get caught and that will end up costing you thousands of dollars.

You can use Flickr.com (free image sharing site) images if you search for commercial use only images and you must always attribute the owner of the photo with their name and a link back to their Flickr page.

If you are looking for more free places for images, Entrepreneur.com has a good article on this;

http://www.entrepreneur.com/article/238646

Just make sure you read the license agreements of all the sites you are taking photos from. Not all allow ad hoc usage of their photos.

When it comes to image placement, I like to put a small image formatted into the first paragraph of text, aligned to the right.

Here is an example:

SEO Campaign Case Study: 1,117 Social Shares and 15% More Organic Traffic (In 2 Weeks)

by Brian Dean | Last updated Sep. 23, 2015

"If we're going to make this a success, we have to put a spin on it and make something different." **-Mike Bonadio, star of today's case study**

This example comes from;

Backlinko.com

A great resource on SEO, especially backlinking and off page SEO. His content pieces are always really well formatted. You can see the example article link here;

Backlinko.com/seo-campaign

Now, a small SEO strategy you can use with images is to rename the image files themselves as your keywords. I like to use my long tail keywords in my image file names.

Obviously, again, don't call an image;

Teeth-Whitening-Denver.jpg

If it's a picture of a whale.
If there is a long tail keyword I want to target, I'm happy to use it as my image file name. I rename my images like this;

best-coffee-dallas.jpg

This again use to have a bigger impact on SEO than it does now but it still gives you a small on page SEO boost and it takes all of 30 seconds to do.

Now, let's get into media.

When I talk about media, I am talking about images, infographics, videos, etc. One of the easiest ways to add media to your site is to embed a YouTube video into your content.

Again, make sure the video is relevant. Most YouTube videos allow you to embed their video into your content. This is a great way to get people to spend more time on your site.

There is some suggestion that having a YouTube video in your content can give you a slight ranking boost, but I don't really buy into that much.

It's more for user interaction and giving your readers more value. This is definitely not a must do strategy at all, just something to think about.

Now, with formatting;

Formatting doesn't need to be difficult at all. Nice, even spacing between paragraphs, use sub headings to break up the content and to use for long tail keywords, break up the page with images and media that's relevant to your content and bold important words or sections of sentences, without over doing it.
That is the general outline I use.

Always make sure you are using correct spacing between paragraphs and make your paragraphs no more than 3 or 4 lines long.

Anything more and it becomes a nightmare to read a lot of text.

Let me show you a great example of a well formatted page.

https://moz.com/blog/million-dollar-content

They have images, media, great spacing, nice use of sub headings to break up the content, bolding of important words and just a general great flow to their content.

Importance Factor: 9/10 – Usability And User Interaction Is Now Becoming A Massive Part Of Google's Algorithms. Images & Formatting Also Play A Major Role In Conversions, IE, Getting People To Take The Desired Action On Your Site.

Content Freshness

It stands to reason that content that is updated more often and is more fresh is going to rank better. Google looks at content freshness. A piece of content written 5 years ago and something on the same topic written a day ago has an advantage, especially in certain niches.

That's not to say your content from 5 years ago is still not up to date, it very well could be, but if it's not, you should be updating this content when needed.

Even if it is still up to date, it's still a great idea to add in new sections with any new information. There is usually something else that you can add in that you have learnt over the years.

This mostly goes for blogs and blog content, but can be used by all businesses.

You don't need to write a new piece of content to make your content look fresh again in Google's eyes, but you will need to add or change a significant portion of the text.

I can't tell you how much, as no one really knows for sure. You also should not be updating it for the sake of updating it or changing the words around to make it look a bit different.

You should be looking to update your older content with add on content or major edits, especially if you notice that your rankings are slipping.

Google doesn't want to display static sites in industries or niches or on topics that change. SEO as a topic is an example of that. Things change very quickly.

If you are writing epic content, look to add extra content to that piece every year. You will start to notice slow, but steady improvements in your rankings.

A lot of SEO and being good at SEO is just doing the small things right. Doing the things other people don't know about or are just not willing to do.

When you are updating your content, you should also be looking for new internal links you can point to this new content and of course vice-versa. Links from fresh content seems to have more power or weight behind them and that works with internal links and inbound links.

Give your content a face lift, give it some new links and even do a bit of promotion for it again.

Send it out to your Facebook page, Twitter feed, email list, contact some more people who you may not have contacted last time about your epic or useful content.

You will see quite steady and real improvements by doing this. If you want to go really in depth with content freshness, check out this Moz article;

https://moz.com/blog/google-fresh-factor

Importance Factor: 7/10 – While You Certainly Don't Need To Update Your Content Constantly, By Adding Fresh Content To The Pages You Are Really Trying To Rank, You Give Them A Much Better Shot At Getting A Ranking Boost By Adding In Some More Fresh Content.

Part #3 - Site Wide Ranking Strategies

So we've talked about what you should be doing on your pages that you want to get ranked, but what about the site as a whole? This is massively important.

It's all well and good to have your pages and content on your site perfectly optimized, but you don't want to then suffer at the hands of Google because you've made site wide errors.

What do I mean by site wide?

I mean at a domain level. YourDomainHere.com. So this is what I'm going to teach in this section.

- Why registering your domain name for longer than 1 year can make your site look better in Google's eyes.

- The benefits of either having your domain name registration information public or private.

- Why you should always use the .com extension for your domain name. (Exceptions do apply and I explain those).

- How to speed up your site so it loads quicker for Google and of course your visitors. This is a massive ranking factor right now.

- Why having your contact information on your site is super important.

- How to make your site mobile responsive. Google launched an update giving responsive sites a boost in their rankings.

- How to setup a sitemap, Google Webmaster Tools and Google Analytics.

Domain Registration Length

When you go and register or re register your domain name with your domain name registrar, more often than not, you will register it for 1 year.

Google has always looked at your domain names age, IE, how long has your domain name been actively registered for. There was and still is a big market for aged domain names.

While I don't recommend going and buying an aged domain name, there is something you can do to make your site look more legitimate in Google's eyes and that is to register your domain name for 2 or more years when you first buy your domain.

It can also help when you re register / renew your domain name as well.

Back in the day, a lot of people tried to game the search engines by buying bulk domain names for 1 year, usually exact match domains, throwing some content up on their site and hoping a few of them started to rank.

That was profitable for them, even if only a handful of sites out of that bulk lot ranked, they would make money.

Google wised up and a part of that wising up is them looking at domain registration length. If you register your domain for 2+ years, that in Google's eyes gives you a bit more credibility.

How much of a boost it gives you is hard to say in exact figures. Some people say it helps when your site is really new, that it gives you more credibility in Google's eyes. I tend to agree with this.

If someone is spending the money to register the domain for many years to come, it stands to reason they are planning on doing something more worthwhile on the domain then putting up junk content.

I always register my domains that I know I am going to build on for at least 3 years. I use Namecheap.com for all my domain name registrations.

They are cheap, reliable and easy to use.

Importance Factor: 7/10 – It's Not Something That Will Make Or Break Your Site, But It's Just Another Simple Strategy You Can Add To Your SEO Tool Box That Will Make A Difference.

Public Or Private Whois Information?

When you register your domain name, you have to put in your correct information. Your name, address, phone number, etc.

This is important.

If you put in fake information, there is a chance you could lose your domain name. I understand why some people don't feel comfortable sharing that information, but if you are running a business, it's a must.

People, Google included, can see your whois information. Whois information is when someone looks up your domain names registration information.

The best way to explain this is for you to do a whois search yourself. Go here;

Whois.domaintools.com

And type in your domain name or a friends domain name. Any domain name will do. Leave off the Http://www.

Now, one of two things has happened for you. Either you see their information, or you see something that says that their whois is protected.

Most domain name registrars allow you to protect your whois information for a small yearly fee and a lot of sites use this feature.

I use it on a lot of my sites that I'm not trying to really do any SEO for. It's not a big no no to cover up your information at all.

However, in saying that, having your whois information available is something Google looks at. It's not a massive ranking factor and you are still going to be able to rank even if you do protect your whois information, but unless you have a really good reason to do so, leave it available.

It's no different than having your contact information available on your site. All businesses with a physical presence should be leaving their whois information unprotected.

Why would you protect your information? People who build a lot of sites for a living often protect their information so their competitors can't tell what is theirs and what is not.

For the majority of people and businesses, you should be leaving your whois information unprotected, IF SEO rankings are important to your site.

If you are not trying to rank your site, then protect the information all you want.

Importance Factor: 6/10 – Google Loves Transparency And Having Your Whois Information Available Is Another Level Of That. It's Not Going To Make Or Break You, But Unless You Have A Good Reason To Do Otherwise, Leave Your Whois Information Available. It Also Saves You A Few Dollars A Year In Fee's!

Always .com?

Should you always register and use the dot.com version of your domain name? Yes, with a few exceptions.

There are hundreds of new domain name extensions out there now and I know it's tempting to try and register the name you want in one of those, but this is a dot.com world and will be for a very long time.

Your visitors know dot.com over anything else. So while it's tempting to register;

YourBusinessName.XYZ

You would be better off sticking with the dot.com, even if it means having to find something that isn't as great as what you could register with .XYZ.

Google still looks at dot.com as the major domain name extension and as I said before, so do your visitors. No one is typing in, YourBusinessNameHere.XYZ.

Their first instinct is ALWAYS dot.com.

Now there are exceptions to this. If you live in a country outside of the US and your major customer base is in your country, then you should be registering your countries main domain name extension.

That doesn't mean you can't register the dot.com and have it as a backup so no one else can get it and you could also just direct people from that dot.com domain to your actual site.

If you live in Australia for example, get the .com.au. If you live in the UK, get both the .co.uk and the .uk. If you live in Canada, get the .ca. If you live in India, get the .in. The exception is the USA.

Don't register a .us. It's not worth anything.

Make sure you use and own your own countries top level domain extension for your businesses domain name. Very important not just for your customers / visitors, but for SEO.

You want to be ranking for your countries version of Google and having your correct countries domain name extension is the first step towards that.

Importance Factor: 8/10 – Don't Try And Get Fancy With Your Domain Name, Especially If SEO Is Important To You. Register A Short, Descriptive Dot.com Domain Name That You Are Happy With Over Any Other Extension (With Exceptions).

Speed Up Your Site Quickly

The speed of your site is important for two main reasons.

A) Visitors who come to your site and see nothing load or the site takes longer to load then it should will click away, especially if they are coming from a search result.

B) Google has placed an importance on site speed. Sites that load slower than other results are at an immediate disadvantage.

It makes sense.

When you click on a search result and you are waiting for second after second to see something load, what pops into your mind?

Are you annoyed? Are you considering clicking off the search result?

If you do stay, how willing are you to continue on the site if everything loads slower than average?

I click off pretty quickly and statistics back that up. 47% of users expect a site to load in under 2 seconds.

http://www.aykira.com.au/2014/04/importance-website-loading-speed-top-3-factors-limit-website-speed/

So what can you do to make sure your site loads quickly? First thing you need to do is find out how fast your site does load and luckily, Google has you covered.

You can use their free tool here;

https://developers.google.com/speed/pagespeed/insights/

Simply type your website address into PageSpeed Insights and it will tell you how fast your site loads and what the reasons are for any slowness.

It gives you a score for mobile site speed and desktop. Usually desktop will be faster. If you are below 70/100 for mobile and below 80/100 for desktop, you have a problem.

You are going to need to take these results to your webmaster and show them what Google suggests you fix.

The easiest things to fix are;

Optimizing Images
Leveraging Browser Caching

One other issue you should be looking at to fix pretty quickly is reducing server load time, if PageSpeed Insights says you have this problem.

That will come to down to the website hosting you are using.

Any other errors, unless you are great with HTML and CSS will need to be fixed by your webmaster or someone will some knowledge in these areas.

Make sure that before you do any changes to your website, that you have a complete backup of your site in-case anything goes wrong.

One of the big issues people have with their site loading speed is not compressing the images on their site. This can literally make the difference between a fast and slow site.

If you have multiple images on your site / page that are really big, IE 300kb or higher, you are putting a lot of strain on your website hosting that you don't actually need to.

All images should be compressed before being put on your website. You can shave seconds off your loading time.
I simply use a free tool, which you can find here;
https://compressor.io

Upload your images to this tool and it will shrink them in file size, (not actual viewing size) while maintaining the quality.

Use the compressed images over your old images and you will see a major increase in site load time with just this one little tip.

Now when it comes to another common issue, leveraging browser caching, if you are using Wordpress, this is easy to do, otherwise you will need to speak to your webmaster about this.

Why is this so important?

Browser caching stores your webpages resource files on a local computer when a user visits a webpage.

So basically, their browser stores a version of your site in it's cache so every time the visitor comes back to that page, it will load quickly as it's not having to be re loaded again from your server.

This is something you should be implementing and I will show you how for Wordpress later in this book.

The next thing you need to think about is your server response time. This is basically how fast your website hosting is loading your site.

While it's a pain to have to relocate your site to new website hosting, often it's a must if you want to see improvements in your SEO.

You are going to have a hard time ranking for any sort of competitive keyword with a sluggish to slow site, especially if your competitors sites are much faster.

Why go to all the effort of doing everything else listed in this book and not do this? A lot of people / clients get angry when I say they need to change their hosting provider, they don't quite get it.
Speed is important.

If the PageSpeed Insight tool says your server response rate is lacking, this has to be done. This usually needs to be done if you have purchased cheap or low quality website hosting or you don't know who hosts your site as someone has set this up for you.

If someone has done this for you and your site is loading slow, you should be demanding they upgrade you, especially if you are paying them monthly for this, which you most likely will be.

What kind of hosting should you go for?

That really depends on how big your site is and how many visitors a day you are receiving. It also depends on where you are in the world.

I'll cover this now.

If you are in Australia, serving an Australian audience and you want to rank in Australian Google, (which you should want to), you should be using a website hosting company with a server in Australia.

Same goes for any other country.
I won't give you a recommendation for a hosting company, I will however point you to a site that reviews website hosting.

http://www.whoishostingthis.com/hosting-reviews/

You will be able to find something in your budget range here. If in doubt, ask your prospective hosting company questions.

Tell them about your website, tell them how many visitors you get, ask them where their servers are located. Shop around. Where you host your website is a major decision.

If you want to learn about literally everything you can do to speed up your site, this link has you covered;

https://gtmetrix.com/leverage-browser-caching.html

Importance Factor: 9/10 – If Your Site Loads Slowly, You Are Going To Have A Hard Time Getting Any SEO Traction. The Very Least You Should Be Doing Is Optimizing Your Images.

Contact Information

A site without contact details or any sort of identifiable information looks suspicious to Google and rightly so. If you have no about us page, if you have no email address listed, if you have no phone number or stress address or business name attached to your site, why?

Answer this question.

Why would a website have no contact information?

What was your answer? I bet you thought it was sketchy at best. You would be right. That is how the majority of people would think and the same goes for Google.

If your website has no human presence, it's what I call a 'ghost website'. Ghost websites usually have little value and are only built to gain rankings quickly and profit quickly without usually adding much value to the world.

If you are running any sort of business, the bare minimum you should have on your site is the following;

- An about us page, preferably with images of the owners or some information about the owners or people who work here.

- A contact us page, preferably with a phone number and definitely with an email address or contact us form.

- Directions to your business if you are a retail business or have some sort of physical presence.

- Your business name should be in the footer of your site.

That is the bare minimum for any businesses website,

If you are a blogger or run some sort of content site, you SHOULD be creating a detailed about us page. Give your site an owner. What legitimate website have you visited where there isn't a detailed about us page and a way to contact the people who own the site?

If your site is flagged for any reason with Google, this is the first thing they will look for. If they can see you are a real business with real people behind it, you are making yourself look legitimate in Google's eyes, because you are legitimate.

Same goes for customer experience. I won't purchase anything online unless I have a well defined way to contact them and a detailed about us page.

It's also annoying when a retail or small business does not put their phone number or physical address on their site. I have to go looking for it in Google which sometimes, quite honestly, I won't do and I'll move on to another business.

It surprises me daily that people are still not providing their contact details for their customers, like it's some sort of secret.

Importance Factor: 8/10 – This Is More About Common Sense Than Anything Else. If You Feel The Need To Hide Your Contact Details, Your Trust Level Plummets And That Is Something Google Looks At.

Mobile Responsiveness Is Now Massive

Old HTML sites are not responsive. Most Wordpress sites are. What do I mean by responsive? They change to suit the device they are being viewed on.

If you are viewing your website on a mobile phone and your site is not responsive, it will look exactly how it does on a desktop computer and that usually means it doesn't fit into the device you are viewing it with and it will look awkward and clunky and often unusable.

Why is this important? Because Google made the responsiveness of a website a ranking factor in early 2015.

You can check with Google if your website is responsive here;

https://www.google.com.au/webmasters/tools/mobile-friendly/

If you find you do not have a responsive website, it's absolutely critical that you get this fixed ASAP.

This doesn't usually involve getting a whole new site developed. You can just get a mobile site developed separately, which will automatically redirect mobile visitors to this new mobile site.

This is something you can discuss with your website designer and should cost no more than $100 to $200 dollars depending on the size of your site.

Any recently created website will more than likely be mobile responsive. If not, it is something you need to fix. Don't spend many hundreds or thousands fixing the problem, it should not cost that much.

You can even do it yourself with the help of a paid tool;

http://onbile.com/

Importance Factor: 10/10 – This Is Simply A Must Have In Today's Online World. Half Or More Of The People Coming To Your Website Are Coming From Some Sort Of Mobile Device And If That Experience Is Poor, They Will Simply Move On.

Not To Mention That Google Uses Responsiveness As A Ranking Factor Now As Well.

Sitemaps / GWT / GA

This is the basics of good Google friendly SEO. Creating a sitemap, setting up Google Webmaster Tools and installing Google Analytics on your site.

Creating A Sitemap

A sitemap is a file or document you put on your site that lists all the pages on your site. It helps search engines crawl and find all the pages on your site better and quicker.

It's a really important function to have on your site and you want to submit this in your Google Webmaster Tools account.

It's a very simple and quick process and I have a step by step guide for you below on how to do it;

http://www.wordtracker.com/academy/learn-seo/technical-guides/how-to-create-sitemap

Google Webmaster Tools

This is where Google can talk to you about your websites search health. Google can send you messages through your Google Webmaster Tools account.

This is especially useful if you are unsure if you have a penalty or not. Google sends notices to your Webmaster Tools account if you have received a manual penalty.

This is also where you can go to submit a reconsideration. It's an important account to have.

https://www.**google**.com/**webmasters/tools/**

This is also where you can go to submit your websites sitemap.

It also gives you updates on where you are ranking for keywords as well as a rough metric of how many clicks per day you are getting from Google and your click-thru rate.

Google Analytics

Google analytics is a free analytics tool that shows you how many visitors a day are coming to your site, where they are coming from, what pages they visit, how long they stay, what time of the day they came and a bunch more really cool stuff.

This is very very helpful to building a great SEO site in my opinion. This kind of data is invaluable.
Here is a step by step guide to setting up Google Analytics and more about the functionality on offer.

http://www.wordtracker.com/academy/learn-seo/analytics/set-up-google-analytics

Importance Factor: 10/10 – This Really Is The Basic Fundamentals Of A Solid SEO Strategy For Google And Something You Should Be Doing.

Part #4 – User Interaction Ranking Strategies

Google uses how visitors interact with your site as a ranking factor. They want to make sure their users are having a good experience and if your website provides a poor experience, they want to know this.

It makes sense.

Google is trying to create the most user friendly search engine possible.

Some will cast doubt on that claim and say they are more about profit and they could be right, but none the less, Google provides a very reliable, steady stream of traffic to those who play by their rules.

There is no other search engine that comes close to Google in the amount of traffic they can deliver, so it's wise, if you are looking for search engine traffic, which is of a high quality and 'free', to play by their rules, whether you like them or not.

So in part #4 of this book, I'm going to teach you two things;
- Why user engagement is a massive ranking factor and how you can improve your visitors experiences on your site.

- How having advertising on your site could be costing you rankings and what to do to fix it.

Engagement Is Key

I've already covered in some detail about how users engaging with your site is a rankable factor in Google's eyes. What I want to do in this section is just go a little deeper and talk about a few major engagement factors.

They are;

Pogo-Sticking & Bounce Rate

&

SERP CTR

When I say pogo-sticking, what I mean by that is when someone does a search in Google and they click on your site but they almost immediately or close to it click the back button to go back to the search results.

This tells Google that your site is either poor quality or not relevant if this happens on a continuous basis.

Bounce rate is similar.

Bounce rate shows you how many people in % form are coming to your site and not viewing any other page on your site other than the one they landed on.

I will be putting bounce rate and pogo-sticking in the same category here. You can find your bounce rate data in your Google Analytics account.

SERP CTR is the amount of people who do a search for a keyword you are ranking for in Google and click-thru to your site. This is shown as a % in your Google Webmaster Tools account.

You can find that in your account under; Your site on the web" > "Search queries".

If your listing is getting clicked on less than the average that Google expects, it may suggest your page is not relevant.

So let's start with bounce rate.

How can you improve your bounce rate / reduce pogo-sticking?
(I should mention that not all metrics like this by themselves should be deemed 'bad'. Google takes a lot of things into account when ranking your website. I am simply touching on a couple of the basics that do make a difference to your SEO and your user engagement.)

Here are some suggestions to improve your bounce rate and stop the pogo-sticking.

Obviously, having good useful content that is relevant to your visitors search phrase will make a big difference here. I don't need to go into much detail about this, but this is a must.

Site speed is another big factor.

For every second your site takes to load, you are losing visitors who are bouncing back to Google looking for another site that loads faster. You could have the best, most relevant content in the world but few people will read it if your site doesn't load fast enough.

In the same vein as site speed is site design.

If your formatting is off, if your navigation is clunky and hard to use, people will click off your site almost immediately. I know I do. I won't read a wall of text or read a page that doesn't load properly in my browser, no matter how relevant it might be to my search request.

Which brings me onto another point, which is, making sure your site is mobile responsive.

If I go to your site and it doesn't load properly on my phone or my tablet, I'm going to click straight off, even if you are the most relevant search result.

Excessive advertising and popups is another thing that will cause a high bounce rate or pogo-sticking. If all I see is a wall of ads when I hit your site, I'm leaving, same goes for intrusive popup windows.

If every time I view a page on your site I'm hit with another popup window or slide in or whatever you are using, I'm leaving as well. You should set a timer on your popups so they only display every once in a while to a returning visitor.

So what should your bounce rate % be? These are some industry averages and should not be taken as gospel.

Online Retail Sites – 20% to 40%
Content Websites & Blogs – 40% to 70%
Service & Small Business Sites – 10% to 30%

Now let's talk about SERP CTR.

This is a pretty crucial statistic. If you are in position #5 of Google for a keyword and your CTR is 2% when the average is 5%, Google looks at this from a relevancy stand point.

Even if your page is super relevant to the search result, if your CTR is low, this is something that you will need to fix.

Obviously, there are times when you rank for keywords that are not exactly that relevant and you shouldn't be adjusting anything for those keywords.

If however you check your Google Webmaster Tools account and see that you are ranking for a keyword that you want to rank for and your CTR is lousy, you will need to fix this and often enough it's a fairly simply fix.

First, let's look at what kind of CTR you should be getting in what position.

Position #1 – Around 30% CTR
Position #2 – Around 13% CTR
Position #3 – Around 9% CTR
Position #4 – Around 7% CTR
Position #5 – Around 5% CTR
Position #6 To 10 – Around 3 to 4% CTR

So what can you do to fix your CTR? The first thing you should be looking at is your title of your page as this is the first thing people see when they are looking at your listing.

Is your title relevant? Does it make you want to click on your link? Have a look at the listings around you. Does yours stand out? No?

The easiest way to make your title page more relevant is to put your keyword at the front of the title in some form. If your keyword is; Teeth Whitening Denver, your title could be something like this;

Teeth Whitening In Denver From $77 | Business Name Here

That would make you stand out wouldn't it?

Next thing you want to look at is your description. Are you writing an appealing description here? I've already covered this earlier in the book so I won't go over it again.

Appealing title with an appealing description is often more than enough to boost your CTR. Just do the basics right and you will see results.

That pretty much goes with all SEO.

Importance Factor: 10/10 – Bad User Engagement And Poor CTR Will Spell The End Of Your Sites Rankings, Especially For Any Moderate Competition Keywords.

Ad Placement Can Seriously Hurt You

Google released an update to it's algorithm in 2012 that started to penalize or punish sites with excessive advertising, especially advertising that was considered top heavy.

Top heavy basically means before you can see any content on the page you have to go through a bunch of advertising. This doesn't make for a great user experience for anyone and Google knew that and it changed the way it ranked websites accordingly.
If a user cannot find your content through all the advertising, they are not getting the best search result in Google's eyes and it makes sense.

Advertising above the fold that pushes content down the page is a big no no. What do I mean by above the fold?

Here is Wikipedia's definition

"Above the fold is sometimes used in web development to refer the portions of a webpage that are visible without scrolling."

If you have to scroll down the page before you see any content, everything above that is called above the fold. If all your above the fold space is filled with advertising, that makes for a poor user experience, hence the Google update.

So how should you place your advertising on your site? Let me give you a quote straight out of Matt Cutt's mouth, Google's head of web spam;

> *"We understand that placing ads above-the-fold is quite common for many websites; these ads often perform well and help publishers monetize online content.*
>
> *This algorithmic change does not affect sites who place ads above-the-fold to a normal degree, but affects sites that go much further to load the top of the page with ads*

to an excessive degree or that make it hard to find the actual original content on the page.

This new algorithmic improvement tends to impact sites where there is only a small amount of visible content above-the-fold or relevant content is persistently pushed down by large blocks of ads."

If you keep this in mind while putting advertising on your site, you should be fine. I personally never have more than 3 ad blocks on any of my pages.

My advertising placements are usually; up the top in a banner form, aligned in the content itself, clearly defined of course and in the side bar on the right.

Importance Factor: 8/10 – While You Should Be Thinking About Squeezing As Much Money Out Of Your Site As Possible, You Should Also Be Thinking About How Intrusive This Advertising Is And Of Course, Keeping In Mind Google's Algorithms As Well.

Part #5 - Off Page / Linkbuilding SEO Strategies

This is what most people think of when they think about SEO, backlinking. They just want you to tell them about secret backlinking strategies.

You know the strategies.... the ones all the gurus keep to themselves, the ones that Google will never find out about.... just tell me those ones.

I get asked that constantly.

Seriously, constantly.

Well, I'm here to tell you, there isn't any. Now I'll wait for the conspiracy theory comments....

Unfortunately, there is no quick and simple magic backlinking strategy that always works and always will and that will rocket you to position #1 for any keyword of your choosing.

There are strategies that are grey and black hat that do work, (black hat means against the rules set down by Google, grey hat means straddling a very fine line between acceptable and not acceptable) which will eventually get you penalized by Google and there are strategies that take time and effort and work for the long haul.

Those are the ones I'm going to teach in this section.

Let me say this however. There are no backlinking strategies that will work at all unless you do everything else I talked about in this book first.

No backlinking strategy is going to help you if you don't have a set of defined keywords to target.

No backlinking strategy is going to help you if your on page SEO is sub par and no backlinking strategy is going to help you if your site doesn't appeal to your visitors or is not relevant to the keywords you are trying to target.

Ok, now that's out of the way, here is what I'm going to teach in this section.

- How you can find and use your competitors backlinks against them. Perfectly legal and above board, in fact, it's one of the most common advanced backlinking strategies there is.

- How to use social media for SEO rankings with your epic and useful content. Facebook likes are huge and Twitter shares are also big in terms of rankings.

- Social media is great to get your content noticed, but you can also get a lot of really great backlinks as well with your useful and epic content through email outreach.

- Guest posting is nothing new, but I'm going to show you a way to do it better than the rest to get traffic and great high quality Google friendly backlinks.

- The best of the best strategy part #1 is about getting your site listed where it should be. This won't work for every website, but it will for the good majority of them, especially if you have epic or useful content on your site.

- The best of the best strategy part #2 is about rewarding those who are doing a good job and getting rewarded back with great quality backlinks and social shares.

While backlinking is not the be all that ends all for SEO, good backlinks give you a major boost over your competitors. There is also nothing 'wrong' or 'blackhat' about these strategies either.

Using Your Competitors Links Against Them

If your competitors have backlinks, surely some of those sites linking to them would want to link back to you as well correct? Makes sense?

If you have better information or offer a better service or product, it only makes sense that some of these sites will want to link to you as well.

Well, there is a very simple way to find your competitors backlinks. Now, before I start, I want to say that not all backlinks are created equal.

The tool I'm about to show you will give you pretty much all of your competitors backlink sources.

Some of those backlinks will be rubbish and not worth your time pursuing and while I'll give you some guidance on what to look for, do keep that in mind.

Also keep in mind that 2 or 3 quality backlinks can boost a page from no where onto the front page. With this tool, what you are looking for are a few quality websites to get backlinks from.

So in this section, I want to show you the tool I'm talking about and how to use it to your advantage by finding quality backlinks.

The tool in question is called Ahrefs.

http://ahrefs.com/

More specifically, their Site Explorer tool;

https://ahrefs.com/site-explorer

All you need to do is put your competitors website into that search bar and it will spit out all the backlinks pointing to your competitors website.

Now you can do this for their entire domain or just a page on their site. The tool is not cheap, but there is a limited free option. You can pay per month, but to be honest, there is not a lot of need unless you are going to be using it all the time and most likely you won't need to do that.

Now their free version is very limited, but as I said, you don't need to worry about that thanks to the good people on Fiverr who offer this service for you.

Fiverr is an outsourcing service, very popular and one that I use all the time. People do jobs for $5 basically. If you go there and type in Ahrefs, you will find a lot of people offering to do the work for you for $5.

So you don't need to pay for the tool monthly, just use a Fiverr service or pay for the tool for one month. I have the tool myself, but there is one person I've used before on Fiverr;

https://www.fiverr.com/alekscupid/give-you-full-ahrefs-report-on-any-10-sites

Otherwise, do a search for 'Ahrefs' on Fiverr and look for the providers with the most reviews.
These providers pay for the service and you just pay them for their time. All above board, it just saves you from having to pay as much for a one time use.

Most providers will do the entire top 10 of Google's first page for you. You just need to provide them with a keyword or set of links you want evaluated.

The best way to use this tool is to work out what keyword(s) you are trying to target for what page on your site, do a search for that keyword and look at the first 10 results.

Make sure to skip any sites like business directories or websites like YouTube. You are just looking for your direct competitors.

Before I go any further, if you are interested in using this tool and you should be, you should definitely check out their YouTube channel as well.

https://www.youtube.com/c/AhrefsCom

They give some great tutorials on how to use this tool and on SEO in general, I highly recommend you check it out.

Again, what you are looking for here are websites linking to your competitors that you can go and request a link from. Let's say for example that you are a local business, you are a restaurant and you can see one of your competitors is getting a link from a local food blog, why not ask them to link to you as well?

Send them an email, tell them about yourself and get them to link back to you.

Let's again say that you are a local business, a dentist and you can see a lot of your competitors are listed in the same 3 business directories. Go and get these directories to add you to their listings.

This works well and I do it quite often for clients.

Now let's say you run a blog on fly fishing and you have an epic piece of content on casting. It's the best article on this topic and you notice that your competitors are getting links back from a few different fly fishing websites in their resource section.

These websites are linking back to your competitors and calling them the best websites on fly fishing. Go email these websites, show them your content and ask to be included on their website.

You don't get unless you ask.

The idea here is to find your competitors best links and get them to link to you. This is the corner stone of advanced link building. It's time consuming yes, but simply the best way to get backlinks of quality.

Never go and purchase backlinks. I'm sure that didn't need to be said, but I said it anyway. Unless you are an SEO expert, purchasing backlinks is going to leave you in a bad place in the long run.

You can also outsource this work to a virtual assistant, but that's a topic for another book.

This tool also helps you work out whether or not the keyword you want to target is viable. If you see a good chunk of your competitors have a lot of really good backlinks, you may want to use that to work out the competition of the keyword.

Ahrefs isn't the be all that ends all for backlinking, but if you can pick up a handful of high quality and relevant backlinks, that is often enough to move you to page #1 on Google for your keyword and often enough to put you right up the top of page #1, especially for low to medium competition keywords.

The key to using Ahrefs profitably is to find out where your competitors are getting their links from and find out why these websites are linking to your competitors.

All you need to do then is to replicate those areas on your own site. Find out where and then find out why and replicate.

You should definitely check out this video as well by the guys at Ahrefs on "stealing" your competitors traffic.

https://www.youtube.com/watch?v=WJG-4THsYMo

Importance Factor: 10/10 – If You Know Where Your Competitors Are Getting Their Backlinks From, You Can Work Out Whether Or Not That Keyword Is A Rankable Keyword. Ahrefs Also Allows You To Mimic Your Competitors Backlinking Patterns. If You Can Do This And Then Out Do Them With Your On Page SEO Work On Your Site, You Can Quite Literally Rank For The Toughest Of Keywords.

Social Media Outreach For Epic & Useful Content

Social media has become a big ranking factor over the last few years. Google hasn't really discussed why or how much it helps your rankings in any detail, but ask any SEO professional and they will tell you it gives you a big boost.

From my own results from my sites and my clients sites, social media has the power to rank your pages for very tough keywords.

The two I mostly focus on are Facebook and Twitter. Sure, there are others and they overall do give you a boost, but Facebook and Twitter are streets ahead.

Facebook likes and Twitter shares are what I try and get for every piece of useful content or epic content. Facebook has a way of boosting your rankings overtime and Twitter seems to hold a lot of sway with Google, so when you combine them together, they work fantastically.

I wish I could tell you how many likes and shares you need to rank your pages for, but it's impossible to know, due to many factors, mostly your competition. Having more than your competitors is usually a good start.

If you want to find out how many Facebook & Twitter likes and shares your competitors have, you can use this tool below;

http://www.seoreviewtools.com/social-authority-checker/

There are quite a few tools that do a similar job, so if for some reason this link no longer works, do a Google search for something like 'social authority checker'.

This tool also gives you a rating of authority, which you can use to measure which of your competitors has the best social profile. You can of course, use it for your own sites to see how well you are doing.

97

Now before you do any sort of outreach for likes and shares, you need to make sure your site is setup properly to get those.

Have you ever been to a site like BuzzFeed or a news site where on the page, they have a little bar or maybe a floating bar on the page that asks you to like or share this page on social media?

You want one of those on your site. You want to encourage as many people reading this page to like your content and your pages.

If you are using Wordpress, this is easy to do.

There are plenty of social media plugins that you can add to your site in a matter of minutes. It really doesn't matter what one, as long as Twitter and Facebook are there and it looks good.

I use;

http://codecanyon.net/item/easy-social-share-buttons-for-wordpress/6394476

Now, if you have a HTML site, it's a little more difficult to do as you will need to know HTML to be able to do it. I'd recommend having your webmaster do it.

Here is a script you can use for HTML sites;

http://codecanyon.net/item/facebook-likeboxtwitter-slider/1153760?s_phrase=facebook&s_rank=25

You want people to be able to come to your site and be able to share your content and like your content. Every like and share adds up and over time you are gaining a lot of extra SEO boost for no extra work.

But let's get to the good stuff. How can you get a lot of shares and likes for your content quickly?

I'm going to go in depth on this with an exact strategy in another section shortly, but the main idea here is to ask.

Find people in your industry with a social media following and let them know what you have. It's not revolutionary at all, but it works. Most people simply won't do this.

Let's say you have a piece of epic content on playing online poker tournaments. It's the greatest content freely available on the web, now what?

You want to get as many shares and likes as possible.
Obviously, you tell your own Facebook and Twitter pages about it, but what next?

This is where you want to go for outreach.

Using the example above, I'd go and do a search in Google for any terms related to online poker strategy, tournament poker strategy, etc, etc. You probably already know who the big players are in your niche.

Find as many websites as you can on your topic, make an excel sheet of the data, and you simply ask them to send out your link to their Facebook or Twitter followers. It doesn't matter how many followers they have, it all counts.

Here is a sample email you could send;

"Hi 'Name'

My name is Shane David, I'm a massive fan of your site. I was just reading your article on 'insert topic here' the other day and I know it's going to have a massive impact on my game already, especially the part on 'insert ah ha moment here'.

I've been playing poker now for about 7 years and I started my own poker training site a few months ago.

I just recently wrote an article on 'insert topic here', and I was hoping you would give it a read over and tell me what you think!

I think it would be highly beneficial to your readers as well, so feel free to share it on your Facebook or Twitter page. I'd also be happy to answer any questions your readers have as well.

Again, thank you so much for your great content, I'm a big fan!

All the best,
Shane David"

The idea here is to show them you are not just some random spammer. You know them, you know their site, you know their audience. You want to build relationships with people in your industry.

I know this seems too simple to work, but it does. It's so simple most people don't do it or simply try to complicate things.

Just ask.

If your content is good enough, most people will share it. A share is nothing special to them, but it will be huge for you.

The more social signals each rankable page on your site gets, the higher they will rank in Google and it will also have a positive effect on your site overall.

Importance Factor: 8/10 – Social Signals Are Becoming Huge And Will Only Become More Important Over Time.

Backlink Outreach For Useful & Epic Content

This is going to be a very short section as it follows on from the previous section. You now know how to get social love through social outreach but what about backlinks back to your site? How do you get someone to link back to your site? This requires them to actually have to go into their site and update it with your link somewhere on one of their pages.

Let's say you are a retail business and you sell curtains and you have an awesome piece of content on; 'How To Choose The Best Curtains For Each Room In Your Home'

It's a really good piece of content and now you want to get some links back to your site for all your hard work. You now know how to find your competitors backlinks and you now know how to search Google to find the kind of sites you want linking back to you, but how do you actually get them to link back to you?

You make it as easy for them as possible. Let's say you find a great website to get a link from your competitors links you found earlier, this is a sample email you could send;

"Hi Insert Name Here, (Always personalize)

My name is Shane David, I'm the owner of "X curtain store" and I also write a lot of really good content on curtains on my blog at;

insertaddresshere.com

It's a culmination of all I have learnt in the past 20 years in the industry.

I see that on your page called "insert title here & link" that you are linking to a site about how to choose curtains. It's a very good article, but I've written something which I think is much more comprehensive based on my X amount of years experience in the curtain & blind industry.

You can read that article, 'title here' at the link below;

insertyouraddresshere.com/article-here/

It covers, 'insert brief 2 paragraph synopsis here', and I think your readers would find it very useful.

If you would like to link your page to my article, I've included the html code for you below.

"Insert fully formatted HTML code here that they can just paste into their site".

If you have any questions, don't hesitate to contact me anytime.

All the best,
Shane David

InsertWebsiteHere.com"

Importance Factor: 8/10 – Email Outreach For Backlinks Is Still The Most Valuable & Simple Way To Get People To Link Back To Your Site Manually.

Guest Posting With A Twist

This isn't going to be the definitive guide to guest posting, there are so many of those out there already who would do a better job. In fact, here are a few tutorials on guest posting that are just amazing;

https://blog.kissmetrics.com/guide-to-guest-blogging/

http://backlinko.com/the-definitive-guide-to-guest-blogging

http://www.quicksprout.com/2013/04/01/how-to-get-your-guest-post-published/

If you are unaware of what guest posting is, it's when you write content that you want to get published on someone elses website.

They have the audience you want and in return you give them a great piece of content for their website and they allow you to link back to your website in that content.

That's the very basic version of guest posting.

In terms of SEO, guest posting is a very old technique that Google actually clamped down on. They clamped down on a certain aspect of guest posting I should say.

Marketers were basically creating rubbish pieces of content and spamming them all over the web on article directories and fake blogs. It was just a mess.

So Google cracked down.

Real guest posting however lives on and is still very powerful.

Real guest posting is about writing a piece of content for an authority site in your niche or industry (and only that one site) and providing value.

The benefits of guest posting to you are, you put your name in front of a new audience, you get a backlink back to your site and you get traffic.

And what did we learn from the previous section? Traffic turns into social shares and social shares turns into better rankings.

People come to your site from your guest post and they read whatever link you send them to and they like your page. This works well for both information sites and those who are selling products.

In this section I'm going to show you a very simple way to make guest posting work even better. I call it the shotgun approach.

I'm not going into the basics of guest posting here, I'm talking about one specific strategy. If you want to learn how to do the in's and out's of guest posting, read the links I supplied above.

Most people trying to do guest posting struggle to get any sort of traction because they are thinking too small. If you go and contact 1 person who has a website you want to guest post on and they say no, and you quit, you fail.

BUT

If you go and contact 100 people, you are going to get a few yes' out of that lot. This is where most people get stuck and end up failing. They don't want to put the time or effort into this and therefore they get poor results.

So here is a very effective guest posting strategy. Keep in mind, a few high quality guest posting backlinks can boost your rankings to page #1 very quickly.

Step #1) Find 5 possible guest posting spots.

We want to start with just 5 and go from there. We don't want to spam the entire web right now, we want to be surgical. If we get a no or no response, we find another 5 sites.

You basically want to find 5 people who say yes, starting from the best in your niche.

These are websites in your niche that you think would be open to accepting good quality content on their sites. That's pretty much all of them.

If you want to get a rough idea of the amount of traffic a site is getting, you can use this free tool;

http://similarweb.com

Just type in the website address you are looking at and it will give you a pretty good, if not a little rough indication of the amount of traffic it is getting per month.

There is no hard and fast rule on how much traffic a site should be getting. If they have an audience that you would like to come to your site, that's a good start!

Using the poker niche, there are literally hundreds of quality websites that are dedicated to teaching people how to play poker better or even just poke news sites.

This will work for pretty much every niche or industry.

So your first step is to find 5 of the best. You want to read their website, understand what they do, understand who runs it. Get a feel for them.

You also want to find the best email contact address for them as well.

Step #2) Come up with 5 different ideas for pieces of content.

When you contact these people for a guest post, you want to contact them with an idea, not an article. Explain to them the type of article you want to write, explain to them your expertise.

What I do is I come up with a title, a 50 word synopsis of what I'm going to cover and the 5 major bullet points I'll be covering.

Obviously you will need to be able to write these pieces of content if they agree.

You want to make the title of your proposed article something very attractive and you want to use your bullet points to give them an idea of what you will be covering.

You want 5 different ideas here.

Let's say I had a poker blog on playing online No Limit Hold Em tournaments and I also had a product for sale on that topic, here is a sample article concept.

Title: 12 Strategies To Be The Constant Chip Leader By Mid Tournament With NLHE MTT's

Synopsis: Using my 12 years experience playing NLHE MTT's online, I've come up with 12 air tight strategies to give you the best odds of being chip leader by the start of the middle of any NLHE tournament online.

I'll teach;

- Why playing too tight early on can hurt your chances later in the tournament
- Why you need to be prepared to bust some tournaments early to win more in the long run
- A strategy that makes playing pocket pairs profitable even with a raise behind
- Why being dealt JJ, the deadly fish hooks, is almost a curse when playing early in a tournament
- A simple strategy to chip up before the bubble without having to go all in

Not a bad little guest posting packet if I do say so myself.

Step #3) Contact your desired websites.

Now you want to make contact with your desired spots to guest post. I've written a sample email in a previous section on social media outreach which can be used for this as well.

You want your email to sound personal and not boiler plate. The idea with the shotgun approach is that a lot of people will say no, or not respond.

Now, if they say no, mark them off your list.

Send them a thank you email and move on. Make sure to send them a thank you email for their time. You should probably keep an excel spreadsheet for all of this data.

Who you have contacted, when you contacted them and what their response is, if any.

If you get no response, send a follow up email about 10 days later asking if they received your email. If they don't respond, move on again. Don't worry about the thank you email this time.

So if one of the sites you contact either says no or doesn't respond, you can now use that guest posting idea for another website.

Just keep going until you find 5 that say yes and I guarantee you, if you do this right, 5 will say yes. It really is a simple process of elimination.

Step #4) Write the content

To say you need to make sure this content is of a high quality would be an understatement.

In terms of content length, you should have that conversation with the website you are guest posting on. I like to keep my content around that 1500 to 2500 words in length mark.

Sure, you could outsource this content, but I would be making sure that anyone you outsource this to had the knowledge to write a compelling piece of content.

Preferably you should be writing this material yourself.

It very much is worth it in the long run, not just for the backlinks, but the exposure. The exposure can often be enough to launch an online business, blog, E-commerce store, etc, etc.

The best way to use this guest posting opportunity is to link back to a page you want to rank for, not your home page. If there is a certain page on your site you really want to rank for, link to that.

Often you can link to both your home page and another page in your byline. This will give you two links back to your site from a very relevant source.

You literally cannot buy this sort of powerful link. As long as you write something that is better than what is already out there, you will never run out of links or guest posting spots.

Never.

Step #5) Repeat the process every 4 months

Every 4 months I would be repeating this process, contacting those who have said yes and also contacting those who you have not had a chance to reach yet.

This could quite literally be your only source of backlinks and you wouldn't need much else, it's that powerful. It is definitely a long term strategy, but highly effective.

Every important page on your site could get a massive boost with this guest posting technique.

Importance Factor: 7/10 – The Key To Successful Guest Posting And This Is Where Most People Get It Wrong Is To Use A Shotgun Approach. Contact As Many People As You Can Until You Get 5 Yes' And Then Repeat The Process Over And Over Again With Different Sites, Different Pages And Different Content.

The Best Of The Best Strategy Part #1

This is such a simple strategy but one no one seems to use it. It works over and over again and the backlinks you generate from this method are of an extremely high quality.

You will also generate traffic as well from the sites linking back to you. It will work for most blogs and even for business websites if you have good enough content.

The method is simple.

Lists are a huge on the Internet. The top X. The best X blogs. The best websites on X. The best articles on X. These are the types of lists you need to get links from.

Let's say you have a blog on travel and you are looking for links. Here is an example of a best of the best list;

https://www.flipkey.com/blog/2014/11/03/top-25-solo-female-travel-bloggers-to-follow-in-2015/

If you ran a travel blog for females, wouldn't you want to be on this list?

Not only is it targeted towards your audience, so you will be getting highly qualified traffic if you are on this list, it's also a very, VERY high quality backlink, back to your site.

There are often dozens if not hundreds of these types of lists in all niches and industries, you just have to know what to search for.

You would want to be searching for terms in Google like;

Best travel blog
Best female travel blog
Best travel articles

Best travel blog for singles

Whatever you can think of that is relevant to all your content on your site, or even just one piece of content. You might have a travel blog in general, with one piece on traveling the world as a female, by yourself.

The article could cover everything from best destinations to security precautions you should take and now you want to get as many links as possible from relevant sites.

Maybe you write on Poker and you want to get your blog some high quality links. Same thing applies. I typed into Google;

"Best Poker Blogs"

And dozens and dozens of lists turned up, like this one;

http://www.yourhandsucks.com/poker-blogs/

BuzzSumo.com again is a good option for you as well. It will show you some of the more socially popular search results for your search terms.

You basically want to get your site listed in as many of these best of the best lists as possible.

Now that you know how to find these types of sites, how do you get your backlinks back to your site? I've already talked a bit about this in previous sections, but it comes down to email outreach.

Two ways to do this.

The first way is to look at these lists and look for broken links. A lot of the time these lists will have links to sites that no longer resolve or work.

If you can find a few of these, you are almost guaranteed a link back and the way I do it is simple. I contact these websites and I politely let them know they have a broken link and I suggest my link as a replacement.

A little cheeky but it works really well.

I'll even go as far as to give them the HTML code they can copy and paste with the link to the exact page I want linked to.

Anything I can do to make it easier for them to link to me.

The other way to do this is to simply contact them and explain to them why your site or article should be linked to on their list.

Keep it short and to the point, explain the benefits, explain what your content does better and how it's relevant to their site or list.

There is nothing more to it than that. The 'secret' here is knowing what sites to look for to get those high quality backlinks and I've covered that in quite a bit of depth already.

Importance Factor: 7/10 – This Is A Very Simple Way To Get Backlinks And Traffic From Relevant Sites.

The Best Of The Best Strategy Part #2

With this strategy you are the one who is going to be linking to other websites. Sounds strange I know, but reciprocity is a powerful tool to employ, especially when it comes to backlinking.

This method will not only get you a lot of links back to your site, but also a lot of social shares. I'd say the amount of social shares you will receive from this strategy will greatly out do your backlinks gained, but that's not a bad thing.

While social shares on platforms like Facebook & Twitter are not as powerful as a good backlink, they are still very powerful and a lot easier to get.

It's also a good thing to have some diversity in your backlink profile. It makes it look more natural in Google's eyes, because well, it is!.

A mixture of backlinks and social shares is becoming the norm for high ranking sites and with this strategy, they are both quite obtainable.

What I want to show you is a very easy way to start getting relevant backlinks to your site. That method is resource pages.

It's nothing new, but it's something most people don't use and you can pretty much use this for any business type, blog, niche or industry.

A resource page is where you link to other websites and mark them as a great resource for your readers to go to. Kind of like the last backlinking strategy but in reverse.

A resource page could be something as simple as a page on your site that links to other websites with a central theme. For example, you might have a blog on cupcakes and making cupcakes.

I bet there are other blogs on cupcake making that you read, so why not share these with your readers.

You could create a simple top 10, top 20, top 30 list of the best cupcake blogs that you read and why you read them, what they offer, that sort of thing.

Then you go and contact these blogs and you let them know that you linked to them and why. People love to be mentioned.

Especially in context of "the best". They get flattered, they share the list on Facebook and most of the time, if they are webmasters, they will point a link back to your list.

If possible, create as many of these lists as possible. I did this for a client who was in wedding supplies.

We created top 15 lists for all the different wedding industries in their city. Wedding venues, wedding cake makers, wedding photographers, wedding dresses, celebrants, reception venues, you name it.

Anything to do with weddings, we found the best businesses and we created separate lists on them all and we contacted these businesses and let them know.

This client ended up with over 30 great backlinks, 12,000 Facebook likes for their various pages and a lot of new traffic coming to their website.

There is no downside here. You are guaranteed some love back and you are guaranteed to make some great new contacts.

To create these types of pages, just create a new post (if you are using Wordpress) or a page for each top list.

Don't just give out a link, explain what each business does, why you are linking to them with their contact details and of course, a link back to their site.

Give each business 50 to 100 words of unique content in your description of them. Make it useful to your readers.

Importance Factor: 7/10 – This Is A Very Easy To Way To Get Backlinks, Social Shares And Make Very Useful Contacts In Your Industry. You Can Set Something Like This Up In An Afternoon And Have Traffic And Shares By The Next Day.

Part #6 - E-Commerce Ranking Strategies

So I've covered a lot about general SEO strategies that any site can use, now I want to start talking about some more specific strategies for specific types of sites / businesses.

In this section, I am going to talk about two ways you can boost your E-commerce style sites SEO. If you have a shopping cart and are selling physical products online, this section is for you.

These strategies will even work for affiliate style E-commerce sites.

In this section, I'm going to cover;

- Why long tail keywords are the bread and butter of all successful E-commerce websites. Every successful E-commerce site understands the importance of targeting not just their main keywords, but also the long tail keywords.

- How using longer, unique content for your product pages can boost your rankings in a matter of weeks. Most E-commerce sites tend to use the stock content supplied to them by the manufacturers, this is a big no no.

Long Tail Keywords

While I've already touched on the power of long tail keywords when it comes to SEO, I also wanted to talk about how they can be used for those creating or running E-commerce style sites.

I should mention, every ranking method talked about in this book can be used for E-commerce sites, some are just more effective than others and as always, it begins with great keyword research.

This method is a combination of what I taught in the previous long tail keyword section and also the commercial keyword section of this book.

Ranking product pages for E-commerce sites has always been one of their major challenges. Often there is not a lot of text on the page and often the structure of the site or framework you are using to create your E-commerce website is inflexible and not always the best for SEO purposes.

There is one way to combat both of these issues and that's to target very noncompetitive, yet highly targeted and profitable keywords.

It's hard to rank a standard product page for keywords like 'iPhone Cases', but you can definitely rank a product page for keywords like 'Polka Dot iPhone 6 Cases'.

While there is a lot less traffic for these long tail keywords, they are highly targeted, not competitive and highly commercial keywords and there is a lot more of them!

The more keyword specific you are with your product pages, the better chance you have of ranking. Yes, this means creating more product pages, but in the long run, this is the cheapest advertising you are going to get that is also extremely targeted.

You will be ranking for keywords that people are using to make purchases.

The first step in any E-commerce setup should be your keyword research and understanding that you need to do this in bite sized chunks.

Sure, create a great big content page with awesome content for the big keywords, but don't try and go for home runs with your product pages with little to no content or little to no on page SEO, it just doesn't work that way.

Inch deep, mile wide is always a great motto when it comes to SEO.

Let me give you an example.

Let's say you are selling ice making machines and you have a sub section on your site for portable ice making machines and in that, you have a list of products to sell which do that specific job.

This overall page would be perfect to target a keyword like; portable ice makers, but with your specific product pages, you want to go much deeper.

Now let's say you are selling a 'Igloo portable ice maker', but not just any Igloo portable ice maker, you are selling the 'Igloo ICE103'.

That there would be one of my main keywords. While 'Igloo portable ice maker' gets more searches, the specific model keyword is a lot less competitive to rank for and highly commercial.

People searching for that keyword are much further along in the buying process. That's not to say you don't want to rank for the bigger keyword, but you want to get as product specific as possible.

You want to base your on page SEO around the product specific model keyword. If you sell more than one type of 'Igloo portable ice makers, you may want to setup a specific content page to target that keyword as it's more competitive and will require more content to rank.

Importance Factor: 9/10 – Without Long Tail Keywords In The Mix, E-commerce Sites Become Almost Unprofitable Unless You Are Somehow Able To Rank For Extremely Tough Keywords, Quickly, Which Rarely Happens! Even So, You Should Still Want To Target Long Tail Keywords Because They Are So Profitable And Quick Rankings Are Very Possible!

Unique Content Is Powerful For E-Commerce

Most product pages either have little or no content on them. What content is usually on them is most often copied from the manufacturer of the product.

Which of course means, everyone else in the world selling this product is using the exact same content you are on your site.

It surprises me how many people come to me in my line of work and tell me that they have done really great on page SEO to their site and pages on their site, but none of their content is unique.

If your content is not unique, the chances of you ranking anywhere for any keywords you want to target, is next to zero.

I repeat, next to zero.

This SEO thing is starting to sound like a lot of work right? Absolutely, it is, but the rewards are worth it. An endless flow of targeted buying traffic.

As I keep saying, if you do exactly what everyone else is doing, you are going to get the exact same results or worse. Those results are usually extremely poor.

When you start doing more in depth keyword research like I talked about above and you then add that with good unique content with good on page SEO, that's when things start to happen for you.

So how much unique content do you need and how should you go about it?

I'm going to give you an annoying but correct answer on how much unique content you need per page.

It depends.

It really depends on the keyword, but my motto is, if some unique content is good, more must be better!

The first step is to take a look at your competitors pages for the keywords you want to rank for and see how much content they have on their pages and if it's unique.

Let's take the previous example with portable ice makers.

'Igloo ICE103'

Here is a good example of what one of your competitors is doing content wise;

http://icemakerexperts.com/igloo-ice103-portable-ice-maker-review

For product keywords like this, I would be aiming for about 500 words of unique content, minimum. What type of unique content is up to you.

The worst thing you could do however is put up the default, non unique content you were probably given by the manufacturer.

Find some way to make it unique. Re write it if you have to.

When you add in good keyword research with good on page SEO and good unique content with E-commerce sites, you start to see amazing results.

Importance Factor: 10/10 – For E-Commerce Businesses Who Are New To SEO, Unique Content Is The Easiest Way To Beat Your Competitors. Are There Competitors Ranking Well With Content That Is Not Unique? Yes, Is It Something You Can Replicate, Most Likely Not. This Is A Simple Strategy, That Takes Work, But Works Better Than Any Other Strategy, Especially In The Long Term.

Part #7 – Local SEO Ranking Strategies

I have a book on Local SEO & Small Business SEO ranking strategies out on the Amazon marketplace currently, but I also wanted to add in a few simple strategies directly targeted at local businesses.

I spent a good part of my career to date helping local businesses with their SEO.

One of the great things about Local SEO is if you do the basics right, you are going to be ahead of 98% of your competitors right off the bat.

Most local businesses completely neglect their SEO and or rely on someone who did their website design and 'threw in' SEO as a bonus.

I can assure you now, if you are in that category, your SEO was not done properly. But we can fix that!

Here is what I'm going to teach in this section;

- How to use simple local business directories to get dozens of relevant backlinks in a matter of hours or days. This is the easiest way to get backlinks for a local business.

- Why getting your 'NAP' right is extremely important to Google and to those who are looking for your business online.

Directories Are Gold

When it comes to local SEO and ranking well for the keywords that matter to your bottom line, you don't need a lot of backlinks to make this happen.

Local keywords are very often not competitive and by nature have large amounts of commercial value to your business. The easiest way to get relevant backlinks to your local businesses website is directories. It's not a new method, it's not even a particularly clever method, but it's easy and it works.

This is what most companies who are offering to do your local SEO start with. Nothing more than finding local business directories and getting your website listed in them.

What they will call it, is citation building.

As Moz.com puts it well;

"Citations are defined as mentions of your business name and address on other webpages—even if there is no link to your website. An example of a citation might be an online yellow pages directory where your business is listed, but not linked to.

Citations can also be found on local chamber of commerce pages, or on a local business association page that includes your business information, even if they are not linking at all to your website."

In this section, I want to talk more about business directories and getting actual backlinks to your site. You want to get your local business listed in as many business directories as possible. This will give you a lot of good quality backlinks back to your site.

Below I've listed the top 20 for the US. Every country has their own directories, just do a search for; 'business directory' 'business directories' 'local business directories'

In your countries Google search engine. You will find lots of great directories. You can also find local directories just for your city as well by searching for something like;

'business directory Chicago'

There are tons of great directories. There is not much else to explain here other than you want to get your business in as many FREE directories as you can. I would not pay for a business directory listing. This is more of a bulk approach to backlinking, which is completely safe for local businesses.

So here are the top 20 business directories for those in the US. Also make sure to look for local directories as well.

http://www.google.com/local/add/businessCenter

https://www.bingplaces.com/

http://listings.local.yahoo.com/

https://www.yelp.com/

http://www.angieslist.com/

http://www.yellowpages.com/

http://www.whitepages.com/

https://www.supermedia.com/business-listings

http://www.yellowbook.com/

http://www.citysearch.com/

https://advertise.local.com/

http://www.linkedin.com/company/add/show

https://foursquare.com/

http://www.manta.com/

http://www.hotfrog.com/

http://www.judysbook.com/

http://www.dexknows.com/

http://businessdirectory.bizjournals.com/advertise

https://www.yellowbot.com/signin

https://register.kudzu.com/packageSelect.do

Now, if you want to find citations / backlinks and have them added for you without doing all the work yourself, there is a very good paid tool called WhiteSpark that will do this for you.

https://www.whitespark.ca/local-citation-finder

It will find all the best directories and citations on the Internet based around your business and what you sell and where you are located. I highly recommend it. It's cheap and you only need to pay for it for a month to get everything setup. There is also this list of citation sources from Moz based around specific industries;

https://moz.com/learn/local/citations-by-category

Importance Factor: 9/10 – If You Run A Local Business, This Is A Must Do Step For Your SEO. It's Easy, Quick And Cost Effective.

NAP It!

NAP stands for Name, Address and Phone number. It's an important element of local SEO, especially with Google.

Google wants your site to have this information on your website and they want you to make sure that all the directories you are listed in also have your correct or updated NAP.

It helps their users when your information is correct.

Google also uses this data when they are ranking your website. Geo targeted information like this is used by Google to make sure you show up correctly, when local keywords are searched for.

In other words, you want to make sure you have this information freely available and easy to see on your website and you want to make sure every directory knows about it.

It seems like a pretty simple thing to do and that's because it is, but you would be surprised just how many small and local businesses don't get this right.

So here are a few steps you can take to make sure this is working for you.

First thing is to make sure your NAP is on every rankable page on your site. Every page you want Google or your visitors to find, needs to have this information on it.

The easiest way to do this is to put your NAP in the footer of your site. If you don't know how to add content to your website, ask your webmaster.

With Wordpress, it's much easier. You only have to add it once to your Footer.php file.

It doesn't matter how you do it, or if you use abbreviations like AVE instead of writing avenue. Just make sure your Business Name, Phone Number and Physical Address are listed on your site.

But what if you have multiple locations?

That's a little bit tricky, but not a lot more so.

You can put all your NAP information together for all your locations, that's not a problem at all. If you have 2 or 3 locations, put them all in your footer section of your site.

But what if you have 10+ locations?

I'd recommend setting up a small page on your site for each location with each individual store's NAP on it. How some of my clients have done this is to take a photo of each store's location, write a few words about the store and staff and also include your NAP on the page.

Worried about privacy? Maybe you work from home? Leave off the street address. It's not ideal, but it works.

Another important thing to make sure is fixed up, especially if you have changed locations is to make sure all the business directories you are listed in have your correct information.
Google uses NAP for the purposes of relevancy and you want to make sure your website ranks for the locations you are currently in.

You also want to make sure it's the same information that you input into your Google My Business account. (What use to be called Google Places).

Make sure you update this ASAP.

Importance Factor: 9/10 – Simple, Simple Little Strategies You Can Implement That Will Give You A Big Advantage Over Your Competitors. NAP Is Super Important For Any Local Business.

Part #8 – Wordpress Ranking Strategies

Wordpress has made building sites so much easier for the average person. You don't need to know a lot of HTML to be able to build a nice looking site with Wordpress.

Wordpress however, straight out of the box, is not the greatest for SEO. It can be clunky, slow, code heavy and overall just not the best for perfect SEO.

But luckily with Wordpress and their range of plugins you can tweak your blog / site so you can have the level of SEO you need to beat your competitors.

In this section I'm going to be talking about the following three strategies;

- The plugins you should be using for great SEO. Plugins can be a bit of a catch 22 at times. The more plugins is not always for the better, in fact, I recommend an extreme plugin diet if you are serious about your SEO.

- A few simple Wordpress tweaks that you can do just to give you a little bit of a boost. These little 1% boosts all add up.

- How to speed up your Wordpress site. Wordpress can be extremely clunky and resource heavy, but with the right settings and plugins, you can make your site lighting fast and this is a huge ranking factor.

The Plugins You Should Be Using

Wordpress makes life easier, it has a lot of functionality to offer, but it's also a bit overwhelming when it comes to plugins.

I've always gone with the theory that more is less when it comes to plugins. You don't need EVERY plugin created to run a great, SEO compliant Wordpress site.

In fact, it can be quite detrimental to your sites speed.

Plugins have a tendency to use a lot of resources and make a lot of requests from your hosting. They also are one of the main ways hackers get into your Wordpress site.

That's why it's so important to make sure your plugins are of the latest updates and you only use reputable plugins to begin with, but that's a whole other book right there.

Right now, I'm going to give you a list of the most important plugins you should be using on your site for SEO and just all round general purposes. I will also explain a little bit about each and how to use certain plugins for massive SEO benefits.

Over time, some of these plugins might stop getting updated or better options may become available, so always make sure to do your research first.

All the plugins below are free as well and you can find them by name in the Wordpress plugin directory.

Wordpress SEO By Yoast

This is the most essential plugin for SEO for any Wordpress site. This plugin allows you to change settings in your Wordpress dashboard that greatly benefit your SEO.

In this book, I will not be showing you step by step how to use this plugin, but I will be giving you the resources you need to learn exactly how to do so yourself.

I will however be talking about some settings you should change on your site in a chapter coming up and you can do those changes with this plugin.

Wordpress SEO By Yoast gives you the ability to change settings in your Wordpress site without having to know any sort of programming.

Wordpress out of the box is not ideal for SEO. There are a lot of issues with titles and tags and indexing of duplicate content.

Here is a great article and video on how to install and setup Yoast perfectly.

http://www.wpbeginner.com/plugins/how-to-install-and-setup-wordpress-seo-plugin-by-yoast/

WP-Optimize

Overtime your Wordpress database will get quite big and it will start to slow down your site. This plugin will help you optimize your database so it stays small and efficient.

WP Smush

WP Smush compresses your image files without a lot of degradation so they load quicker. Speed is super important to Google rankings, so this is a must have plugin.

WP Super Cache

Designed to create a cache of your site so that when visitors return, they are shown a much faster loading page as they are being shown a static HTML version of the page, not a slow loading Wordpress PHP version.

Super helpful for those who have slower hosting and for some reason can't or don't want to move web hosts.

BackWPup

I can't stress how important it is to make sure you backup your website often. Every time you make a sizable change to your site, you should make a backup of it in case anything goes wrong.

With a backup, you can restore it to the point where it was working.

Google Analytics Plugin

This plugin lets you put in your Google Analytics code once and be done with it. Otherwise you would have to put the analytics code manually into your header file. If you know how to do this, you don't need this plugin.

Akismet

Helps to block out comment spam on your site. Unless you are running a blog style site, I'd recommend turning Wordpress comments off, especially for small and local businesses. If you turn comments off, you don't really need this plugin.

Advanced Lazy Load

Another plugin that helps you load images in a better way. Advanced Lazy Load only loads an image on your page if the visitor scrolls down to it. Without this plugin, all images must load before the page is displayed properly.

This gives you an option to delay that loading time and get your page loaded fast. If you have fast hosting and or not a lot of images, you don't need this plugin.

Wordfence Security

100% free security plugin for Wordpress. It will check to see if your Wordpress site has been infected by any trojans and will run in the background and protect you from intrusions. It can slow your Wordpress site speed down a bit and it does eat resources, but still a worthwhile plugin.

CloudFlare

CloudFlare is my favorite CDN (content delivery network). It basically allows you to host files / media on their servers instead of on your own server to take the pressure of your hosting.
It will speed up site significantly and I highly recommend using a CDN. It also has great security features to protect you from Ddos attacks.

-

If you want to learn more about Wordpress, you should absolutely check out this resource below;

http://www.wpbeginner.com

If you want to learn how to make Wordpress work for you, there is no better resource. Very user friendly and not a lot of technical jargon used.

Importance Factor: 10/10 – You Need These Plugins To Run A Wordpress Site For The Best Possible SEO, Unless You Are Familiar With Coding. These Are The Plugins I Use On All Of My Wordpress Sites.

These Small Wordpress Tweaks Make A Huge Impact

In this chapter I want to give you a few simple Wordpress tweaks that will help you get more out of your Wordpress SEO.

It won't be a big chapter, but these are all tweaks you should be doing to get the most out of the benefits Wordpress gives you when it comes to SEO.

Let's begin.

If you are not running a blog style website, I'd suggest turning comments off. It's just not something you need to deal with.

It will help with comment spam and help your page speed as well. Here is a video on how to do that;

https://www.youtube.com/watch?v=3_NtlL6VLjg

The next thing you want to do is setup your Wordpress SEO by Yoast to no index the following;

archive pages, categories and tags.

This will help stop a lot of the duplicate content issues that Wordpress has. You can follow the steps I outlined in the previous chapter to do with Yoast SEO. Make sure to read that link I supplied and watch the video.

There are also a lot of really good videos on YouTube on how to setup Yoast SEO.

You will also want to go into your Wordpress dashboard to the settings section, then permalinks and make sure you have it clicked to;

Post name

This will make your Wordpress site look like this;

http://yourdomainhere.com/how-to-build-muscle/

Instead of the default of something like this;

http://yourdomainhere.com/?142

The first option is much better for SEO as you are getting your keywords into your URLS as we have discussed earlier.

Now, in your posts, you want to make sure you use your image ALT tags wisely. This gives you a way to tell Google and other search engines what the images on your site mean and how relevant they are to the page.

Here is a good resource on how to do that well;

http://havecamerawilltravel.com/photographer/image-alt-tags-wordpress

Remember again, to also check out this article below to fully learn how to setup Wordpress SEO by Yoast. It is absolutely required reading.

http://www.wpbeginner.com/plugins/how-to-install-and-setup-wordpress-seo-plugin-by-yoast/

Importance Factor: 10/10 – These Tweaks Need To Be Done. Not Much Else To Say Here!

Speed It Up!

I've talked a lot about your websites speed in this book already, but with Wordpress you have a lot of options to make your site load lightning fast.

A Wordpress site loaded up with lots of plugins or no optimization will run relatively slow, but there are so many options available to you to speed up your site and that's what I'm going to talk about in this chapter.

I'm going to give you a simple breakdown of everything you can do to maximize your sites speed.

First thing you want to do is set a baseline of your sites speed right now and thankfully Google makes that easy for you to do with their Google PageSpeed Insights tool.

https://developers.google.com/speed/pagespeed/insights/

You can run your site through this tool and see what kind of speed your site is running at now to get a good baseline.

You really want your site to be over 70 for mobile and over 80 for desktop. I've already talked about this tool before so I won't go further into it now, just make note of the numbers.

The next step is making sure your hosting is working for you. It's hard to tell sometimes what is what when it comes to speed.

Is it your Wordpress site being sluggish or is it your hosting not keeping up? Google PageSpeed Insights does give you some information on this.

Server response time.

If your server response time is 1.5 seconds or higher over multiple tests on multiple days, you might need to change your website hosting company.

If your hosting is slow, there is not a lot you can do to really speed your site up to where it should be.

If you are paying only a few dollars per month for hosting or not sure what you are paying for hosting or who you are even hosting with, you probably do need to change up.

Now let's assume your hosting is fine, what next?

Next you want to deactivate and uninstall all non essential plugins. Anything that is taking up space for no real reason.

This can be a huge speed suck in itself.

If you have dozens of plugins installed, you are crippling your site. Most of the time you can replace one plugin with another that does the job of two or three.

This is something you will need to investigate on a case by case basis.

When you've worked out what needs to be removed, don't just deactivate the plugins, fully uninstall them and never look back.

Now we want to start using some of these plugins, starting with WP Smush to make our image files smaller, but before you do that, you need to make sure you've already compressed them as I talked about earlier in the book.

You should try and keep image file sizes below 200 kb, if not 100 kb in size. Then you want to run them through WP Smush to compress them further.

If you already have images on your site that have not been compressed, I suggest putting them all through this process immediately and re uploading them.

Next thing you want to do is optimize your Wordpress database with the plugin WP-Optimize.

This will remove all old comments marked as trash or spam and it will also get rid of previous draft copies of posts that have been updated with newer versions, plus it will optimize your database on the whole.

The reason this is important is if your database gets too big, it will slow your site down considerably.

Once you have done that, it's a good idea to go into the themes section of your Wordpress dashboard and uninstall / delete any themes that you are not using.

Again, we want to make your Wordpress site as lean as possible. Just make sure not to delete anything you are currently using.

You also want to make sure any theme and plugins you are using are up to date. Often plugins and themes will release updates that should be updated, which you can do easily in Wordpress.

Make sure to backup your Wordpress site before doing anything that may affect how your site performs.

Now is the time to also setup WP Super Cache. This will help speed up the site even further to return visitors.

Also, if you have a large amount of videos or images on your site, I'd recommend setting up a CDN (content delivery network) to host these files.

This means instead of using your website hosting resources, you will be offloading some of the work to the CDN, which will in turn make your website load a lot quicker.

136

Think of a CDN as a global cache. It serves files using their servers which are closest to where the visitor is coming from. This makes loading these files a lot quicker.

I honestly don't think you need a CDN for local or small businesses. If you are however targeting and getting traffic from around the world, a CDN makes sense.

It also makes sense if your site is image and video heavy. If you are getting a lot of traffic, it also makes sense to use a CDN.

With these few basic tweaks, your Wordpress site should be loading extremely quickly. You want to go test again with the Google PageSpeed Insights tool to see what numbers are you getting now.

If you are still experiencing slowness and your server response time is still average or bad, it most likely is your hosting slowing your site down. That will need to be addressed sooner rather than later.

You may need to upgrade your account to one with more resources or shift hosting companies completely.

Importance Factor: 10/10 – As I've Discussed Throughout This Book On Numerous Occasions, Your Sites Speed Is Hugely Important To Getting Good Rankings.

Conclusion

I've spent the best part of half my life doing SEO full time and I can honestly say, these 39 strategies are the best of the best.

No fluff, no extras, just the best stuff that is going to get you ranking quickly. Remember that SEO is a medium to long term game and that anyone offering you instant or quick rankings should send you running in the other direction.

Each of the strategies above are time tested and proven to work, but none of them alone are magic pills. You need to put in place a combination of them, starting with good keyword research.

If there is only one thing you takeaway from this, please let it be that good keyword research is the absolute fundamental of strong SEO. You cannot have one without the other.

Before you go, make sure you also check out the SEO resource list down below. These are all the SEO resources and tools I use in my business.

Leave A Review On Amazon If This Book Was Helpful To You

First off, thank you so much for purchasing and reading my book. I can't tell you how much that means to me. I started writing as a hobby, as a way to teach what I know to others. It's grown into so much more than a hobby and I have you to thank for that.

If you have 5 minutes, **I'd really appreciate it** if you could go back and leave a review for this book. Tell me your honest thoughts!

Honest reviews are massively helpful to me as an author and as a book seller.

Visit my Amazon author page below;

http://www.amazon.com/-/e/B014GT0Q9K

My Other Books In This Series

If you are looking for more books on SEO written by me, I am in the middle of creating a series on everything to do with SEO, based on my 17 years of experience in this field.

That includes, keyword research, on page SEO, advanced link building, local & small business SEO & SEO outsourcing.

If you like what you've read here, check out the rest of my series at the link below;

http://TheFullTimer.com/My-Books/

101 SEO RESOURCES

The Best Free & Paid SEO Tools & Resources To Out Rank Your Competitors

WEB

ANALYSIS

SITE ARCHITECTURE

ONPAGE OFFPAGE

SEO

CONTENT

Search Engine Optimization

TRAFFIC

RANKING

INDEXING KEYWORDS

BACKLINKS

SHANE DAVID

101 Epic SEO Resources Used By The Professionals

One of the biggest requests that I get from my clients is for my resources and tools that I use in my SEO business.

While there are definitely no secret tools that will make your site jump straight to page #1, spot #1, there are certainly quite a lot of tools that will give you a massive head start over your competitors.

In this section, I am also going to be covering my favorite resources. Articles, tutorials, papers, etc on SEO that I've found helpful over the years.

It's all well and good to have the tools at your disposal, but it's completely pointless if you don't know how to use them or extract the most value out of them.

Each tool or resource will come with a brief explanation of why it's important to me. Not all the tools or resources will be free, but most will be.

You should be looking to pay for your continuing education on the topic of SEO. So let's get started!

My Favorite SEO Tools

https://adwords.google.com.au/KeywordPlanner
Google Keyword Tools – One of the best keyword research tools on the market and considering it's from Google and it's free, you can't really go wrong.

https://adwords.google.com.au/KeywordPlanner

SemRush.com – This is a paid keyword research tool with a limited free option. I love this tool, I would never be without it. It gives you a lot more data than Google will and it's much more than just a keyword tool. One of the major benefits is it's ability to track your rankings.

Http://semrush.com

Ahrefs.com – If you are getting serious about your SEO, you should be getting serious about backlinking and Ahrefs helps you with that in ways no other tools can.

It will show you all your competitors backlinks (if you don't know how powerful that is, there is no hope for you!) and that's just the tip of the iceberg of what this tool can do for you.

Http://ahrefs.com

Open Site Explorer – Is in a similar vein to Ahrefs, as it helps you track your backlinks and that of your competitors. I like both tools and recommend them both, but I prefer Ahrefs right now.

https://moz.com/researchtools/ose/

Google Webmaster Tools – This is basically the control panel to your rankings with Google. Google Webmaster Tools is the nervous system of SEO if you are serious about ranking with Google.

You will get alerts from Google here, you can check your rankings, check your CTR's, submit your sitemap, submit urls for consideration. It's important.

https://www.google.com/webmasters/tools/

Google Analytics – Another great free tool from Google. You need to know how many people are coming to your site, where they are coming from, are they coming from Google or Facebook or Twitter, or did someone link to you?

You need to know how many pages your visitors read on your site, how long they stay for, what pages they read and the list goes on. That's what a good analytics program gives you, and Google Analytics is a good one for most businesses.

https://www.google.com.au/analytics/

Moz Toolbar – I talked quite a bit about how to use this tool in this book already. Moz's free SEO toolbar allows you to see how competitive a keyword you want to target will be to rank for. You can install it in your web browser and do great keyword competition checks all day long.

https://moz.com/tools/seo-toolbar

Google PageSpeed Insights – Another great free tool from Google. Google PageSpeed Insights allows you to see just that, how fast your site loads and if it is slow, what the problems are. This is one of the first tools I use on my clients sites.

https://developers.google.com/speed/pagespeed/insights/

Majestic SEO – The main job of Majestic SEO is to check your backlinks for you and of course, check your competitors as well.

https://majestic.com/

Google Trends – This is something I use often to check for the popularity of a niche or topic. This free tool allows you to see what's trending in terms of searches. You can type in any search query and see how it's trending. Are a lot of people searching for it right now? Do they search for this keyword from a specific country or time of year?

You can see if a topic or niche is trending down over the years before deciding to go all in.

https://www.google.com/trends/

KeywordTool.io – Another great free Keyword research tool, but the paid version is better. It's more about giving you suggestions that you might not have thought of. I use this keyword tool to get suggestions and then I run them through SEMRush.com or Google Keyword Tool.

http://keywordtool.io/

GTMetrix – Another great free tool to help you find where you need to optimize your site to get it running smoothly and quickly. The faster your site loads, the better rankings you will achieve.

https://gtmetrix.com/

HootSuite – If you are doing any sort of serious social media marketing or managing, and you should be, this suite of tools is for you. You can manage all your social networks easily and quickly in one convenient control panel. It's a complete social media manager.

https://hootsuite.com/

Screaming Frog – Great name, great product. Their SEO spider tool comes in real handy when you want to audit your site, your competitors sites or your clients sites. It will crawl your site and tell you about all the errors you have and how to fix them to maximize your on page SEO.

http://www.screamingfrog.co.uk/seo-spider/

BuzzSumo.com – Not so much an SEO tool as more of a research tool. BuzzSumo let's you see what content has the most social shares based on any keyword you input. If you are looking to find a way to replicate epic content already out there, this is for you.

http://buzzsumo.com/

Moz Local Search – If you are a local business and you want to check your local listings to make sure they are all there, this is a great free tool for that.

https://moz.com/local/search

AuthorityLabs – High quality and very accurate SERP tracking. If you want to know where you are ranking at all times in all the big search engines, AuthorityLabs is for you.

http://authoritylabs.com/

SpyFu – This tool allows you to find all your competitors profitable keywords. Whether they are organic or with Google Adwords, you can download all the keywords they are targeting and use them for your own site.

http://www.spyfu.com/

DeepCrawl – If you are serious about your SEO, you know how important auditing your sites performance is. DeepCrawl does just that, it crawls your site looking for any sort of structural errors that will negatively impact your SEO.

https://www.deepcrawl.com/

Incognito Browsing – Every web browser has this functionality and it's so important for checking your rankings. If you continually search for a keyword and click on your site, Google is going to move your site up the rankings, but only for you. This is a personalized result and it throws off your ability to see where you are ranking.

Put your browser in incognito mode and you will see the true SERP results.

Schema Creator – There is no better way to build structured data for your website.

http://schema-creator.org/

Raven Tools – If you are looking for a good SEO reporting tool, this is it. If you do work for any clients, this will create stunning looking graphs and charts showing exactly how they are doing in their SEO efforts. It's also good for your own SEO work as well. It's not cheap, but it's a tool I use.

https://raventools.com/

BrowserShots.org – Every time I do client work, the first thing I do is see how the site loads in all the different web browsers. You would be surprised how many sites look good in say Chrome, but terrible in Firefox. This free tool will show you what your site looks like on dozens of different browser combinations.

http://browsershots.org/

Google Mobile Friendly Test – Check to see if your site is mobile responsive in a matter of seconds.

https://www.google.com.au/webmasters/tools/mobile-friendly/

Compress Jpeg – Image compression website. Just load up your image and let it compress it for you in less than a minute. Completely free.

http://compressjpeg.com/

Compressor.io – Another quality image compression tool which is also free. I've added this as well in case one or the other stops working.

Http://compressor.io

Bitly.com – One of the best URL shorteners on the market. If you want to cloak or track who is clicking on your links, use Bitly. The tracking data is the best part of this tool. Perfect for social media, you can see where your links are getting clicked from and how many people are clicking.

http://bitly.com

Copyscape.com – A simple and free tool that will allow you to check your content and your website for duplicate content. Duplicate content is a big no no, so if you are outsourcing your content, you should be checking it here for any duplicate content issues.

Http://copyscape.com

Whois.DomainTools.com – A very powerful domain whois checker. It gives you a lot more data than other whois checkers.

Http://Whois.DomainTools.com

XML Sitemaps – If you are not using Wordpress and you need a good free XML sitemap creator for your site to submit to Google Webmaster Tools, this will do the trick!

https://www.xml-sitemaps.com/

Piwik – A very good quality analytics program if you don't want to use Google Analytics or you want something more robust. It's free and open source and it doesn't share your data with anyone other than yourself. You will need to manually install it on your site.

http://piwik.org/

Robots.txt Checker – Check to make sure your Robots.txt is working properly and optimized properly. It will find all errors.

http://tool.motoricerca.info/robots-checker.phtml

Wayback Machine – Awesome little site / tool that let's you see what a domain / site looked like in the past. Great for working out whether or not a domain you want to buy has been used before and for what. If it was used for a spam site, you now won't waste your money on the domain.

https://archive.org/

CloudFlare – CloudFlare is my favorite CDN (content delivery network). It basically allows you to host files / media on their servers instead of your own to take the pressure off your hosting.

It will speed up site significantly and I highly recommend using a CDN. It also has great security features to protect you from Ddos attacks.

Http://cloudflare.com

Whois Hosting This – If you are looking for good, reliable and fast website hosting, this site has a lot of high value reviews you can look at to see what will suit your purposes.

http://www.whoishostingthis.com/hosting-reviews/

SimilarWeb.com – Want to see what kind of traffic your competitors are getting and from what sources? SimilarWeb.com is a great free tool for this. There is a paid version which I recommend as well. I use this almost daily.

Http://similarweb.com

Whitespark Local Citation Finder – If you are a local business or you do consulting work for local businesses, this tool is a must. We all know how important citations are to local businesses and this tool will find you the best for your businesses industry.

https://www.whitespark.ca/local-citation-finder

Wistia – High quality business video hosting with great analytics and other video marketing tools thrown in. If you do anything with video, this should be your first port of call.

http://wistia.com

Optimizely – When you start to get serious about SEO, you start to get serious about the results that traffic is bringing you and your conversion rates. That's where A/B testing comes into the picture. Optimizely does this well and it also allows you to offer personalization to your visitors, which can be based on previous actions they have taken.

Really useful tool.

https://www.optimizely.com/

Haro – Help A Reporter Out is a great service where you can register yourself as an expert and when reporters are looking to interview and quote experts in your field, you can send them your information. This is great for building yourself into an expert and also getting great links back to your site.

http://www.helpareporter.com/

Website Penalty Indicator – This tool uses select historical data to see if your site may have a Google penalty. Good tool but only really useful for sites that have been around for at least a few months.

http://feinternational.com/website-penalty-indicator/

PhotoDune.net – If you need good stock photos for your website and let's face it, we all do, PhotoDune.net is a great place to get them. Low price, high quality and run by the guys and girls at Envato.

http://photodune.net

My Favorite Wordpress Tools

It's no secret that I love Wordpress. It's quite frankly the easiest way to design a high quality website. It's not always the best platform for some builds, but for the majority of businesses and blogs, Wordpress is everything you need.

The ability to hotswap themes and plugins makes Wordpress a dream for developers and those who want to design their own websites.

Below are 15 of my favorite Wordpress tools. Most have something to do with SEO, but some are just what I believe to be essential tools for any Wordpress user.

Wordpress SEO Plugin By Yoast – Absolutely the best SEO plugin for Wordpress and it's free. This plugin allows you to fully optimize Wordpress and your content perfectly for SEO.

https://wordpress.org/plugins/wordpress-seo/

Easy Social Share – If you are looking to add those awesome social share bars to your Wordpress pages, this is the tool I use. It's a paid tool, but it offers a lot of flexibility in terms of look and feel of your social bars. There are plenty of free tools that offer less customization available as well.
http://codecanyon.net/item/easy-social-share-buttons-for-wordpress/6394476

Advanced Lazy Load – What this plugin does is it delays loading any images on your site until the visitor scrolls down the page close to them. So instead of loading all the images on your page as soon as they visit your page, which takes time, this plugin delays that, meaning your initial page load speed time is increased significantly.

https://wordpress.org/plugins/advanced-lazy-load/

Wordfence Security – 100% free security plugin for Wordpress. It will check to see if your Wordpress site has been infected by any trojans and will run in the background and project you from intrusions. It can slow your Wordpress site speed down a bit and it does eat resources, but still a worthwhile plugin.

https://wordpress.org/plugins/wordfence/

WP Optimize – Wordpress has a tendency to create very large databases which will slow your site down over time. WP Optimize reduces the size of your database. I run this once a month on my Wordpress sites.

https://wordpress.org/plugins/wp-optimize/

WP Smush – This plugin will compress the size of your images, which again helps with page load speed and also the size of your Wordpress site. All very important. I use this in combination with the other web based compressor tools I talked about earlier.

https://wordpress.org/plugins/wp-smushit/

WP Super Cache – Designed to create a cache of your site so that when visitors return, they are shown a much faster loading page as they are being shown a static HTML version of the page, not a slow loading Wordpress PHP version.

Super helpful for those who have slower hosting and for some reason can't or don't want to move web hosts.

https://wordpress.org/plugins/wp-super-cache/

OptinMonster – OptinMonster isn't exactly a Wordpress plugin, it's a tool / service that allows you to create really great optin boxes and lead capture forms for your site to collect email addresses, which for most businesses, is absolutely crucial.

http://optinmonster.com/

CodeCanyon.net – Again, not a plugin in itself but a massive marketplace where you can go and find thousands of different high quality plugins for sale. This is one of my favorite sites on the Internet.

http://codecanyon.net/

LeadPages.net – Not a plugin per say, but something I use often with Wordpress. LeadPages is a tool that allows you to easily create very pretty and effective landing pages or lead pages to collect email addresses.

Http://leadpages.net

My Favorite SEO Resources

While what I've covered in this book is great, it's definitely a lot of great information and will give you everything you need to start seeing much improved rankings, it's not an entire guide to SEO and it was never meant to be.

If you are considering taking your SEO very seriously, maybe as a career or you really want to create great sites with perfect SEO, then you will need to continue to learn and improve on your skills.

So below, I have put in all the best articles and resources that I have read and implemented. I've found them to be the best of the best over many, many years of research.

Moz – The big daddy of SEO training, learning and news. Moz is the biggest name in SEO tools and articles. If it's happening in SEO, it's being written about here.

https://moz.com/blog

QuickSprout – A blog written by a very successful online entrepreneur, Neil Patel. He doesn't just talk about SEO, but a lot of it is SEO related. Absolutely worth a read.

Http://quicksprout.com

Backlinko – If you want to learn about link building, this is the place. Brian Dean is the king of link building and he teaches you all he knows within his blog. You could spend hours here reading and learning.

Http://backlinko.com

Search Engine Land – Another high quality industry news website. Often more technical than other sites. More for those in the industry.

http://searchengineland.com/

Search Engine Journal – This site has been around since the beginning and is still of a high quality. They talk about more than just technical SEO, covering topics like content marketing, paid search and social media.

http://www.searchenginejournal.com/

Kissmetrics – They offer a range of tools for marketers but their blog is also of a very high quality and a lot of it is SEO related. I spend a few hours a week here.

https://blog.kissmetrics.com/

Linkedin – We all know what Linkedin is, but what you may not have known is that Linkedin has a lot of great SEO groups that you can join and read and interact with. A lot of people are posting daily, really good articles and news related to SEO.

Http://linkedin.com

The links below are to specific articles.

https://blog.bufferapp.com/beginners-guide-to-seo – If you are new to SEO and you want to learn the in's and out's from the very beginning, you should read this ASAP.

https://blog.kissmetrics.com/get-started-using-schema/ - Schema is really important for local businesses, review sites, recipe sites, etc and this article gives you a great primer on how to use it.

https://moz.com/learn/seo/schema-structured-data – Another great article on schema.

http://oliveremberton.com/2014/life-is-a-game-this-is-your-strategy-guide/ - This has nothing to do with SEO, but more life in general and business in general. Really well written and will give you a kick up the bum.

https://moz.com/blog/beginners-guide-to-link-building – A complete beginners guide to link building. If you are new to the concept, give this a quick read.

https://www.distilled.net/content-guide/ - If you have ever wanted to learn about advanced content writing and marketing, this is your guide. It's more in depth than most people would need, but it's brilliant.

https://builtvisible.com/micro-data-schema-org-guide-generating-rich-snippets/
https://builtvisible.com/micro-data-schema-org-guide-generating-rich-snippets/ - Very advanced stuff on schema and generating rich snippets. 99% of this won't apply to you unless you are doing advanced SEO. I included it for the 1%.

https://www.portent.com/blog/internet-marketing/geeks-guide-gaming-algorithms.htm – An interesting take on a geek's guide to gaming SEO and social algorithms.

http://help.outbrain.com/customer/en/portal/articles/1411677-how-to-write-good-seo-friendly-articles – How to write good SEO articles from the powerhouses at Outbrain.com.

http://www.shoutmeloud.com/how-to-write-perfect-seo-optimized-blog-post.html – Same topic as above but specifically for Wordpress. Really good article on on page SEO with Wordpress.
http://backlinko.com/seo-techniques - 21 actionable SEO techniques that you can implement now, from the brain of Brian Dean.

http://www.performics.com/performics-and-roi-study-49-percent-of-mobile-searchers-made-a-mobile-purchase-in-past-six-months/ - If you are unsure why mobile responsiveness is so important, read this article.

https://moz.com/blog/mobile-seo-tips-for-everyone-whiteboard-friday-12429 – A good series of tips for mobile SEO and a good video on the same.

http://www.quicksprout.com/2012/03/29/how-to-optimize-your-mobile-site-for-search-engines/ - Optimize your mobile site for SEO.

https://blog.kissmetrics.com/seo-for-ecommerce-websites/ - The ultimate guide to E-commerce SEO. Must read for anyone building E-commerce sites or doing E-commerce SEO!

https://www.quicksprout.com/university/how-to-optimize-your-ecommerce-site-using-on-page-seo/ - Really great video on how to do great on page SEO for E-commerce sites.

https://moz.com/blog/new-title-tag-guidelines-preview-tool – I've already talked about how your title tags are super important in regards to your SEO rankings, but this article takes it to another more advanced level.

https://moz.com/blog/google-traffic-links – One of my favorite articles of all time on SEO without having to worry about link building.

https://moz.com/blog/1-dollar-per-day-on-facebook-ads – While this book is about SEO, I am a big fan of Facebook advertising for businesses of any size. This article gives a good argument to why you should be using FB ads.

https://moz.com/blog/7-advanced-seo-concepts – Great article on advanced on page SEO concepts.

https://moz.com/blog/google-algorithm-cheat-sheet-panda-penguin-hummingbird – Looking to get rid of and or understand why your site or sites were hit with Google penalties? Give this a read!

https://moz.com/blog/amazon-seo-organic-search-ranking-factors – Amazon has a massive search engine and user base, so if you are selling any sort of products, you should be looking at Amazon as an alternative to Google. Great article on how Amazon's organic search works.

https://moz.com/blog/personas-understanding-the-person-behind-the-visit – One of my favorite articles on understanding persona's of your customers and visitors. It really is more than just keyword research!

http://backlinko.com/17-untapped-backlink-sources – 17 untapped backlink sources by Brian Dean. If you've run out of link building ideas, try these.

http://backlinko.com/google-ranking-factors – One of the best SEO articles of all time. 200 top Google ranking factors. While each ranking factor is not described in a lot of detail, the list itself is pure gold.

http://backlinko.com/skyscraper-technique – One of Brian Dean's most famous articles. The Skyscraper Technique is a brilliant way to gain backlinks and has become a staple of all SEO'ers.

http://backlinko.com/on-page-seo – Anatomy of a perfectly optimized page. Looking for more information on doing great on page SEO? This is it!

http://backlinko.com/keyword-research – A really good in depth beginners guide to keyword research. I'd highly recommend this for anyone struggling with keyword research.

http://www.quicksprout.com/2015/10/26/should-you-outsource-content-marketing-11-questions-to-consider/ - Good questions to ask yourself if you are looking to outsource your content marketing. http://www.quicksprout.com/the-definitive-guide-to-conversion-optimization/ - The definitive guide to conversion optimization by Neil Patel

http://www.quicksprout.com/the-advanced-guide-to-link-building/ http://www.quicksprout.com/the-advanced-guide-to-link-building/ - The advanced guide to link building by Neil Patel.

http://www.quicksprout.com/the-advanced-guide-to-content-marketing/ - The advanced guide to content marketing by Neil Patel.

http://www.quicksprout.com/the-advanced-guide-to-seo/ - The advanced guide to SEO by Neil Patel.

http://www.quicksprout.com/the-beginners-guide-to-online-marketing/ - The beginners guide to online marketing by Neil Patel.

http://www.quicksprout.com/the-complete-guide-to-building-your-blog-audience/ - The complete guide to building your blog audience by Neil Patel.

https://moz.com/learn/local – A great overview all of the different ranking factors for local businesses.

http://www.amazon.com/Small-Business-Local-Ranking-Strategies-ebook/dp/B014GQYBCG – This is my book on Amazon on how to do perfect small & local business SEO.

http://www.seobook.com/blog – Aaron Wall's blog where he talks all about SEO. Aaron Wall is a very respected name in SEO and definitely a blog you should check out. Pull's no punches.

http://searchengineland.com/10-wordpress-seo-questions-took-10-years-answer-214050 – Really good article on Wordpress SEO. Covers 10 very important topics.

https://medium.com/swlh/how-i-got-50-851-views-on-slideshare-and-706-email-subscribers-for-less-than-350-9138a23d18b5#.ytiafb5d7 – Really interesting article on how to use Slideshare to get visitors and get them to take an action.

http://www.jonloomer.com/2015/10/07/facebook-lead-ads-2/ - Facebook is rolling out a new type of advertising called lead ads. If you like to get in early on things, this is a good read.

http://nichehacks.com/easy-ways-to-get-backlinks/ - 3 simple ways to get quality backlinks without doing any 'SEO'.

Get More Up To Date SEO Ranking Strategies

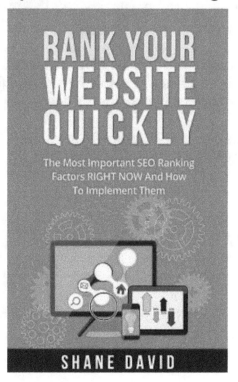

Wait A Minute! Rank Your Website Even Quicker With This *Free Gift*

As a token of my gratitude for purchasing my book, I wanted to give you a small, but very valuable gift. I've been doing SEO full time now since 1998 and I know better than anyone else how quickly things change when it comes to SEO.

But there are a handful of time proven strategies that always work and that constantly rank your website for the keywords that matter quickly.

You can grab your free gift below and implement these strategies today. **Here is what you will learn;**

* The ONE strategy that will almost always guarantee you high rankings
* The new rules of SEO – Google knows more about your site than ever before
* An instant rank boosting SEO strategy that you can implement in minutes

I also give away a lot of great content on SEO. I share all my latest tips and strategies and results, straight from the trenches.

<u>Click on the link below to get access;</u>

http://thefulltimer.com/seo/